THE
INCREDIBLE
SHRINKING
WOMAN

THE INCREDIBLE SHRINKING WOMAN

ESSAYS

ATHENA DIXON

Published by Split/Lip Press
6710 S. 87th St.
Ralston, NE 68127
www.splitlippress.com

ISBN: 9781952897030

Cover Design by David Wojciechowski

Cover Art by Keli Gagen

Man, sometimes it takes you a long time to sound like yourself.
    —Miles Davis

" . . . but the stillness was the sleep of swords."
    —Zora Neale Hurston, *Their Eyes Were Watching God*

Table of Contents

A Goddess Makes Platanos

I am standing in the kitchen making platanos. It is a Friday in the summer and all the windows of my home are open. I am trying to create some semblance of peace today, but you are on my mind. I believe I can forget the bitter of these last years and smash the sweetness of memory between my teeth. I am wrong.

Soon, waiting for the edges of the fruit to caramelize, I am sitting on the laminate floor staring up at the spidering of brown dots from the bathroom leak above me. There is comfort in connecting the splotches into patterns, finding the images in the blank spaces until my eyes ache. I close them and the insides of my lids glow red. This colors the world and for a moment I can forget what brought me to the floor alone, letting the coolness sink into the backs of my thighs. No matter what I think I am forgetting; I know I'm never really alone. My memories are viscous and they settle into me each night, these bones bedding down and fighting a war, lonely for some fat, a sliver of love.

I sleep to the left, so close to the edge I'm nearly falling. When I am bold I starfish my body across the mattress, arms and legs thrown to the four corners of my room. My bottom arches my back from the padding and before long I am curled left again, and morning makes its way in on the backs of birds and garbage trucks. This is life in the city. So different from the sounds of trains or the sort of fog that covers the backyard like a down blanket. I like it here because here I am new. Here I can shed the layers I've crafted over the years and become bare.

In theory, I can be whomever I choose, and this is reflected in the things scattered about my apartment. My old college room-mate once said a woman needs only three things: red lipstick, high heels, and a vibrator. I have all three. But in the end, I am the same as I've ever been. A study in cardigans and Chuck Taylors. A portrait of curls and a bare face. A face morphing into my mother's as the years go by. I am starting to dissect the ways we are dissimilar, the ways we are exactly the same.

To the men in this new city, I am a challenge. Perhaps a puzzle to decode. I am skittish, yet I invite them close enough to see the whites of my eyes and the red painting my lips. Then I disperse into a cloud of songs they can no longer listen to, and into the void erasing me from each of their memories. But from afar I long for them. I hope to curry their favor until they finally see me. What they actually see, I am not sure. It is when I am seen when I am afraid. Not of them, but of myself and the havoc I can bring. I've learned I can spiderweb across a man's life in equal parts love and regret. I'm not easily forgotten, but often left behind.

I become a bridge between things these men want to forget and the lives they desire. Some sort of way station between the men they are and the men they hope to be. I'm never quite enough and yet always still way too much. Too loving. Too clingy. Too good. Too nice. Too hard to pin down. Too irresponsible. Too much off the mark. Too much of a prude. Sometimes these men get caught between what they seek and what they seek to lose, and before long everything has crashed down around us, the dust and ruin of our collective lives now smoldering at our feet.

This pattern of men coming and going is easily traceable throughout my history. Perhaps it is my accommodating personality. Or fear of confrontation. Or lack of connection. Maybe it is my easy swallowing of words that has allowed men to ebb and flow. It is probably all of the above. These men write their names upon the vellum of my skin. This way I can never forget them. I am sure I leave inscriptions of my own. Perhaps it is a bit of melody or a gap in the story. The men's names are not many, still readable but slightly faded. But beneath the thinness of my breastbone, passers-by can see a collection of hearts beating. It is a steady pomp and circumstance that directs my daily movement, slow and plodding and endless.

On the counter above me, I can smell the heaviness of oil from the stove, the platanos now soaking through a layer of paper towels. My stomach ripples to life only to be ignored so I may concentrate on what is important: starvation for something more. My body is heavy. It is thick and full and untouched. I smash it and find myself soft, yielding. It is unexpected. I mash into my skin like the platanos press, trying to mold myself into something these men will love, something these men will remember when they are starving.

Instead, I bruise myself the color of the ripened fruit, a mess that hides the sweetness inside. It's on this edge of rotting where the best is found. But the rot brings flies and wolves. It makes them circle, starving and ready to strip flesh from bone and heart from chest. But I know I don't want to be picked clean. There should be nothing left of who I was before these men. It makes it easier to forget. I want to be devoured so there is nothing left except the memory only on *their* lips and a hunger for more of me.

The Greater Whole

I am cloistered in the tube of an MRI machine in the midst of a sweltering summer. I'm listening to Usher offer to leave his woman for the prospect of something better on repeat while the tech stands behind glass and directs me through a speaker that echoes. *Stay perfectly still.* The metal is cold beneath the thin gown and there's an exposure extending beyond my near nakedness—it is the splay of my body in sections on a screen, and the months leading up to this moment. Months of bone scans, blood work, x-rays, liters of barium sulfate, and IV flushes that make me burn from the inside out.

Months ago, when my friend Charles' car slid softly off Route 183 and into a downy snowbank, the quiet crunch of his bumper was nothing more than another thing to hide from my parents over winter break, a collection of tattoos and a piercing the other things buried deeply beneath the weaving of the woman I was becoming. When Charles and I trudged up the deserted road, our boots muffled in the deep snow, all I could think about was how I would explain the hours away and the trip to campus to take care of business my parents already thought was complete. Weeks later, when my left foot began to balloon, I pinpointed that accident as the cause, no matter how little sense it all made.

By the time I'd finally alerted my parents something may be wrong, I'd lost the sight of the bones beneath my skin. There began the doctors' tales of possible tumors and cancer, blockages in my inner workings that no one could explain, leading, finally, to a foot and ankle clinic across the street from the local Ponderosa where I'd burned the tips of my fingers on the restaurant's steamer tables. Now, in the heat of my fear and the closeness of the MRI, I close my eyes and wish for the massive cooler inside that restaurant, tucked away from the public. It was the perfect hiding place for the days my feet ached in no-slip shoes as I rationalized that being a poor teenager wasn't that bad—the job was certainly better than the one at Taco Bell that I lost because I just couldn't stomach dipping my arms elbow-deep into a sink, washing dishes for anyone other than my mother.

"What I think you have is lymphedema. Most times it's seen in cancer patients, but it can be hereditary. There is no cure."

There are words after this, reminding me to keep my leg elevated above my heart while I am not in motion. What foods to avoid and compression stockings to be fitted for. But *there is no cure* snags all the threads I've built up around me. All my hopes of seeing a needle plunge into my ankle flesh, the fluid inside me bursting forth like a popped balloon, dry up and drift to the ground.

"If we did that it would be like trying to stick a needle in a sponge. It doesn't do anything. You'll learn to adjust."

The doctor leaves me with Meige disease, or lymphedema praecox, a hereditary disorder that often causes lymphedema in childhood or around puberty. He leaves me to discover on my own, via the rabbit hole of Google and WebMD, that my lymph vessels formed without the valves that keep fluid from flowing backwards, which makes it difficult for my limbs to properly drain. He leaves me without much care or concern of just how my life is changing.

My mother and I exit the office into the dense haze of a summer afternoon, settle into her black Park Avenue, and coast back down State Street toward uncertainty. The rest of July begins to unravel into worries for the fall and what I will do once I can no longer hide my condition by wearing the summer's off-brand Birkenstocks and Wal-Mart flip-flops. I can't stop thinking about my father's swollen ankles, compressed and stuffed into house shoes, certain that all of my current troubles ripple out from him. That makes sense in my twenty-one-year-old brain. I reject those compression stockings with everything in me, afraid and ashamed of their beige blandness.

When people think of lymphedema, they think of the morbidly obese. And even though the medical industry considers me just that, somewhere in my head I draw a distinction between me and what probably pops into most people's minds: the lymphedema cases on *My 600 Pound Life*, a woman with massive curtains of fat swaddled around her legs, covered in Ace bandages, bedridden because the skin is sensitive to the touch. Perhaps people would think of me struggling to lose weight in order to undergo gastric bypass. I'm sorry to disappoint them. My lymphedema isn't that dramatic. *My* lymphedema is much more subdued.

When I arrive home, I climb the stairs toward my bedroom where a blue plastic bin of shoes awaits. I scatter them about the nap of the carpet in duos—but still a jumble befitting what's inside me—my favorite pair splayed next to the foot of the bed. Platform, nude patent-leather sandals that wrap my ankle. There is a photo of me, snapped inside my dorm's stairwell, my legs extending out of those shoes until my thighs disappear into a matching mini skirt. My curves, those I'd beg to return in later years, rest in the vee of the stairwell's handrails. My legs are braced for power, tucked neatly besides each other in a beautiful line. The rest of me cowers and slouches as if I'm not quite sure how to handle what props me up for the world.

I press my foot into the left shoe and feel the toe-strap cut into my flesh. I can ignore that discomfort, and so I reach for the strap to secure my ankle. But there is no willpower nor tug at the small bit of elastic that will make the two ends meet. I repeat this procedure for all of the shoes in the bin, eventually tossing them into an ever-increasing pile of memories to be packed away or discarded. I remember the frat parties the semester I bought those shoes, the parties held off campus as punishment for rule violations and banishment, knowing I'd have a way there and no way back, but somehow I still never had to walk. It is hard, even amidst the pain of too-tight straps, to forget how it felt to tower over the room before I became afraid to stand out.

The idea of a needle floats back into my mind. Perhaps a poke and not a puncture is the answer. It would be like juicing an apple, pressing and pulping what's beneath the skin until all inside has filtered out and flattened the hull. On the desk there is nothing sharp enough, just pens and books and paper. My earring posts are too dull to make a real impact; they could never break the surface enough to matter. I squeeze my foot in frustration and pull away to the perfect indent of my fingers in the flesh. I dig deeper, this time into the inside of my ankle, and watch a divot form. The skin sponges softly back to whole. It leaves me wondering what other ways my body has morphed. I make a show of depressing, then watching rise, my foot and ankle. It dawns on me that no amount of squeezing nor morphing will put things back the way they were. I cry until I am hot and sticky on the floor of my bedroom.

In the bathtub, I let my foot bob and float out of the water. I watch my toes emerge like branches of a baobab tree. They are small against the bloated trunk of my heel, ball, and arch. I press my fingertips into the flesh and feel it sink again, then indent, beneath the pads. The flesh doesn't stay that way, and I have the odd satisfaction in knowing my body still retains some of its normalcy even while it is in flux. I keep pressing into my skin, carving shallow pools where the water gathers then empties back into the void, sucked back into the greater whole with nothing left behind.

In the fall, I let the hems of my jeans extend from boot-cut to bell-bottom. I wear them long enough to cover the backs of my shoes, shredding them against the pavement like I meant it for fashion, not for hiding. The platform sandals and chunky loafers that cut across the top of my newly-engorged foot are boxed away. I cannot force the bulk into last year's winter boots, and so the season slogs on in a sloppy mess of tennis shoes frozen by the time evening rolls around. I end up in compression stockings of my own making—doubled pairs of socks to stop the slush and snow from seeping into my skin. I wear white tube socks that leave a ring around my calf beneath thinner ones that are colorful and fun. Stripes and polka dots and zig zags. Argyle is my favorite. The socks are far from beige. They are far from boring and they keep the questions at bay. I can make this compression look normal. The double socks leave patterns as unique as my fingerprints pressing until the swelling gives way to some measure of normal and a bit more illusion of control.

Ordinary History

There has always been my father. No missing nights nor voids in my memories. I have been privileged; that I will never deny. When I say there has _always_ been my father, I mean in my household, sleeping next to my mother nightly, enjoying his Maxwell House instant coffee from the same mug each morning. He preferred his brew in the white Motorists Insurance cup, two tablespoons of the crystals, water to the brim, no sugar, no cream.

My father was my first view of Black men loving. My parents' long-term relationship—turned marriage nine months before my sister's birth—is the foundation I built upon when I decided I wanted love for myself. I knew marriage was an exercise in both the mundane and the divine. My father rose each morning before the sun and strapped on steel-toed boots, filled a thermos, and headed out to the steel foundry, returning in the afternoons covered in soot, the crinkling paper of treats beneath his jacket. Those afternoons I ate greasy, sweet confections, leaning against the kitchen counter, watching his eyes droop while the kettle boiled. I'd watch him sip his coffee and slip into slumber until he descended the stairs to clean the dust of the factory from his skin.

In the early days of my parents' courtship, my mother held jobs at Church's Chicken and Dairy Queen. I'm sure it was not only her, but also the prospect of free breasts, wings, and sundaes that kept my father hanging out during her shifts. And even though she eventually lost one of those jobs over a free strawberry milkshake, my mother and father embarked on a combined life meant to be better from whence they came. Shortly after their 21st birthdays, I came prematurely into the world. After my birth, their lives unfurled into the piecework of manual labor to afford raising the daughter to whom they wanted to give the world. My childhood was a balance of latchkey and Disney World. This is where my loneliness began, in the stillness of my room on Linden Avenue as an only child who wasn't too much of a fuss.

There were times I longed to be a troublemaker, a girl that people needed to place hands on to control. This would manifest later on, as I learned to slip into roles that got me the attention I wanted, no matter how deep the fracture. But growing up, I wanted to be steadied by aunties and cousins along with my parents. Quiet and good do not the ripple make. Perhaps if I would have shouted and fought and spit, I would have felt seen. As I grew, I stumbled into places I didn't belong with men who weren't for me. Perhaps it was my hunger for them to be a fraction of who my father is that drove me to forget myself and accept the scraps I was offered.

Maybe this shapeshifting has been with me longer than I care to admit. I didn't realize that I didn't need to be anyone except the self I'd yet to define. But even in those echoing afternoons before my parents' cars appeared in the driveway, I knew that I was loved both at a distance and up close. Although it was sometimes at arm's length, I knew those arms could easily fold inwards to pull me into an embrace. The lasting effect of all this, I imagine, was that I got used to the buffer between what I wanted, who I was, and what I needed.

Still, I knew my father loved me, and he loved my mother, through the condensing of his lungs caught between cigarette smoke and factory fumes. He loved us through ninety-minute drives to the Cleveland Zoo where we ate potato roll sandwiches and drank Faygo soda in the parking lot before we headed in. And he loved us through music, filling the basement with sound until I picked over the vinyl remains, one day, to cart back to my adult home.

I was twelve when my parents threw a couples-only Valentine's

Day party in that basement. There is a picture of that night, my parents culled in each other's arms, smiling for the flash. In this photograph, they are young. There is no grey hair, no COPD, no closed factories, no Social Security benefits. They are thirty-three and the world is bright.

Sometime after those afternoons in the kitchen, I slow-danced with my father at a wedding. Not mine, but a nameless, faceless woman whose wedding he was DJ'ing. I was a girl still, against ever marrying, clinging to my father's buttoned shirt while he twirled me around. I remember that dance with him in the reception hall, now a state-run liquor store in my hometown, but I'd forgotten the song when my own father-daughter dance came to fruition. On my night, we two-stepped around a room high above the Philadelphia skyline as the city turned down for the night. There is a picture of that evening, too. I am still clinging to my father's buttoned shirt, head thrown back in laughter, and he is beaming at me. In this photograph, I am young. There is no adultery, no divorce, no depression, no exile. I am nearly thirty-three and the world is on the cusp of change.

For my entire life, I have known love between the folds of greeting cards, flower deliveries, hometown newspaper announcements, ruffles of my hair, and pinches of my chin. My father is a man who still carries the tiny slip of paper the nurse handed him the night I was born, the measurements of my birth, tattered and adored in his wallet. He carries my beginnings like a prize. I know my father thinks I am beautiful. He thinks I'm smart. "I raised you to be among the upper echelon," he says when I forget my place in the world. I knew his expectations of education and success as much as I also knew he wanted me to be happy and loved outside of the confines of his shadow. He often reminds me that I am worthy.

It is under this specter of love that I enter into relationships with men who, in theory, should be *The One*. I find bits of my father in each of them. Love of music. Creativity. Height. Affectionate aloofness. Popularity. Shyness. Athleticism. Protection.

Support. All facets of him, but never quite all that he was and still is. It's because I can find traces of him in these men, and the way he loves my mother, that I think if I will just try hard enough, or just transform enough, things will work out in the end.

It is under this haunting of my father that I never quite pay attention to whether the men I encounter are solid or connected. My father once told me, "You date a man's potential. Not what he is in the moment." And it's true. I find scraps of him, cobbled together from memory and a girl's ideal image of her hero, and I want to connect all the pieces while ignoring the cracks in both the suitors and myself. I try to mend two broken halves to make one whole and am always surprised at the disaster it makes. I keep moving around the pieces of my life to make room for the mess, trying to hide it in order to savor what's good or what will feed me. I can never quite remember that sometimes my heart is in starvation mode, still a latchkey kid alone in an echoing house.

No matter the scraps I accept, my father never interferes, never interjects his opinion about the men in my life. He stays silent and listens to me when I am ready to talk. When things finally break down, as they always seem to do, it is then when he says in a quiet voice, "Tina, this is what I think." And I listen. I don't always act, but I do listen and I see myself in his eyes. I am a collage of all he wanted in the world, and he wishes for that to be cherished by a worthy man. The trick is wanting the same for myself, and being able to hold on until it happens.

Loving my father puts me at a disadvantage. I look out into the world expecting tenderness where there is none, finding only the one-upmanship of who can ghost the other first. Love has made me chase men blindly down back alleys littered with red flags, and stand on shores waving at ships that have already sailed. It makes me put on the masks again in hopes that one of them will resonate with someone somewhere. The ripple effect of my father is the hope that one of those men I have let in and around my body will also take my heart and treat them both with care.

My love for my father makes me blind to a past that tells me that maybe this will not be true. In the future, there may not be the solidness of a body next to me sipping coffee or unlacing boots at the side door to avoid tracking dirt into the house. And maybe life will not bring me a partner who will stroll the bricked path of the zoo while his daughter lingers ahead, her fingers stained with BBQ dust and her belly bubbled with cola. But my father makes me hope. He makes me promises even without speaking that this is all possible. There is no way to tell who or what may set them in motion, though I am quite convinced it is out of my hands, long since given up to the universe and whatever luck this girl can find.

Native Tongue

Small-town Black Midwesterners, like me, exist somewhere between the Bible Belt and the ghetto. We hover somewhere between
now and then. And I think we are forgotten. Hours from Chicago,
New York, Philadelphia, and Los Angeles, oft times we are nothing
more than rest stops and waystations on the road to somewhere
new. We are mistakes on the lake and jokes about burning water.

In my hometown, the Amtrak stops once at 3:05 AM. When
you disembark, you land solidly beneath an overpass with chunky
gravel beneath your feet. There is no station, just the small stack
of a platform. There, in the shadow of the Elks, you blend into
the light reflecting from the MLK Memorial Viaduct and you are
assimilated into rural Black life.

We are neither Southern nor Northern. We exist on flats of
farms, along rivers, around bends of back roads, and in tiny out-
croppings across the heartland of this country. Who we are is informed by our Southern grandparents who became first-genera-
tion factory workers or small-town farmers. We are the children
of parents who wanted our hands to be clean, without calloused
and without lines. We are not subway trains or towering projects.
We are the towns where the graffiti laced trains stop, those insular
places where we race the side of the road to get a glimpse of bubble
letters we can scarcely decipher. We are Friday night football and
summer parades down Main Street.

To search for people like me is to look beyond the concrete
jungle and into the distance. It's to revisit those places that seemed
punishment when our relatives were forced from their cities for

vacations and holidays. To know us is to know the slowness that moves faster than can be imagined. It is to know the sourness of rhubarb between our teeth and the call of ducks in a pond. It's seeing our hometowns dying when the factories close and the buildings begin to crumble. It's living life on either side of the tracks. We are the places where Main Street is a dead end. And in the center of this quandary is where I started to get my grasp on my own sense of self.

Back when I was a student at State Street Middle School in Alliance, Ohio, my daily after-school ritual rarely changed. I'd board the bus and bounce alongside my cello in the very first seat, careful to duck fast enough to avoid the occasional pennies pitched from the back. For as long as I can remember, I knew I didn't fit in. And I won't say that's because there was a particular spark that set that thought ablaze. Instead it was a series of omissions and admissions that helped me understand that I really never had a place. One of the popular kids telling me that my tie-dyed short set was corny. Going to prom without a real date. I always felt as if I was straining to be seen and yearning to be heard.

I walked a fine line between obscurity and acceptance. There were popular kids like my orchestra mate, Cedric, a multi-sport athlete, who drove me to school sometimes. He'd thump into my driveway in a brown boat of a car with the trunk rattling and the ground soaking up the sound. He took care of me in other ways, too. Cedric pitched in with another friend, Charles, to make sure I had Valentine's Day balloons delivered to my classroom like the girls with *actual* boyfriends. It is Cedric who is standing beside me in my prom picture, his date somewhere off to the side. Still, when I am asked to remember my youth, there is a keen remembrance of loneliness, of disconnect.

If I'm asked to remember if I was bullied, I cannot wholly say I was. What I can say is that I recall being hit in the head with a penny or two. I can remember being told I was trying to be white, that I was fat, that I smelled funny. I know that during my final two years at State Street, I carried a stick of Teen Spirit deodorant in my backpack because one of the boys sniffed the air every time I entered the room and I was terrified to be a fat Black girl existing in a cloud of stench. What I can remember now that I am solidly in middle age is that the intersection of popularity and Blackness was where I always got lost.

On our bus route, just before my scheduled stop was Greta's drop-off. Her mother, Sherrie, was my mother's best friend. The two of them spent six days a week working the assembly line at the Genie Garage Door Opener factory. Greta and I'd known each other for years via our mothers, but I'm not quite sure she would have considered me a friend. I'd like to think she did. We were loosely bound by the women who took every bit of overtime offered. Sometimes weekends only consisted of Sundays because time and a half and piecework could cobble together a good life back then. Our families never actually owned any of the things our parents made, be it a garage door opener or a train. But we lived across the tracks, not in the metropolitan houses that were our version of the projects. And we had steady income built upon the backs of her mother and my parents. In that way we were kindred. In that way we were connected.

But I wasn't in Greta's league. I'll be completely honest. She was lean and ran track. She was popular. I was round and wore braces with a tongue tied into a slight lisp. I played in the orchestra just like her but was far less cool. I loved *Star Trek* and wore an evil eye bracelet. Our entire 8th grade year, I wore mostly black and drank only cranberry grape juice for lunch. I thought by skipping meals that I'd lose some of my pudge, and in turn I'd be more than the not-quite-Black-enough fat girl, but skipping meals only made me even weirder. There were times that year I spent weekends in a pop-up travel camper with a white friend named Jennifer. She was the only other girl I knew who was also approaching six-feet-tall before we entered high school. Jennifer was just as awkward as me, trying to navigate her way through a sea of middle-class white students while living a less-than-preppy life.

The two of us clung to each other that year, hunkered down in that camper writing burn books and performing voodoo rituals meant to make us popular and svelte. I nearly set my parents' attic on fire with burning angel stationery. I'd read you could rid your life of bad by writing down the problem and setting it aflame. But all I managed to do in that attic was melt the plastic faces of the cast-off dolls stored there. By the time I graduated high school in 1997, Jennifer and I hadn't fought our way out of obscurity or into the in-crowd. As disappointed as we were, at least we made it out relatively free of embarrassment, though I wasn't without my close calls.

Unlike Greta, who ran sprints for as long as I knew her, I'd run track for a single season; really, a single race in which I came in almost last. I was too shy to run flat-out because I was afraid the spandex shorts beneath my blue and gold uniform wouldn't hold all my flesh in place. This fear was only heightened by the two men in the stands yelling about my thickness. It made me want to shrink, so I slowed down. I heard them above all else because the hypersensitivity of chub rub had made my ears perk. Even if the shorts had held it all together, I was never going to win. I was painfully slow and barely made it to practice. It took Cedric ditching his football and track buddies to walk me there several times a week. At practice, I half-participated in the suicides and laps our coach ordered.

Originally, I'd wanted to throw shotput. My parents had refused. I was already taller than the boys and, again, fat. What a horror it would have been if I'd become muscle bound too. I knew my father had played every sport our shared high school had offered, and if I looked closely enough, I could make out his Afro in the black and white photos in the lobby trophy cases. And I knew Black kids like me were supposed to run track. We were supposed to turn our bodies into a blur along the hard clay lines. Turning her body into a blur was exactly what Greta did. But my body wasn't a blur. It was blob rippling beneath track shorts.

Despite my lack of popularity and athleticism, and because Greta refused to shun me anyway, I followed her off the bus some weekday afternoons and into the corner home she shared with her mother for one very important reason. I needed to watch *Yo! MTV Raps!* Had I continued on the bus until my scheduled stop, I would have missed a portion of the show, and that was unacceptable. After school, all I ever wanted to do was somehow transport myself onto that set and rock my hips with Ed Lover and Doctor Dre'.

My father was the local Black DJ. In a town with two segregated Elks clubs, he provided the music for most wedding receptions, family reunions, birthday parties, and special events held on our side of town. There was always some sort of event being held under his *Mr. D* banner. Many weekends of my childhood were spent in the upper room of that social club: a wide-open square ringed with framed photos of Eastern Stars. There, among the rumble of the trains outside, my father hosted fashion shows with clothing borrowed from Dixon's Menswear and Fashion Bug. Locals would strut the T-shaped runway on audition days until the final line-up was culled into couples and a sprinkling of kids. Or there were those Saturdays my father would cart the cast iron film projector from Rodman Public Library and play reels of cartoons for me and other children splayed out on the wooden floor with vellum bags of popcorn and candy. He'd hand-stencil the flyers and invite the world in.

Most of the time, I tagged along with my father on gigs. I'd relieve him on the turntables so he could grab a plate or use the restroom. I learned to use a fader, how to keep the music building and the party going. Because of my dad's steady bookings, my basement was overrun with vinyl records, cassette tapes, and eventually CDs. All of it was housed in avocado green suitcases for easy transport or else rowed upon buckling shelves. I introduced my father to LimeWire a few years later and he moved his skills to mixtapes which he burned onto blank CDs.

Just like Greta, my father was popular. He was cool and well-respected. He had a shag Jheri curl, smoked More cigarettes, and drove a turquoise conversion van complete with a fold-out bed and mini fridge. Years later, that van would catch fire after a mechanical failure and my sister and I would travel to the city impound lot to look at its shell. We'd laugh about how he'd shouted for our mother to call 911. We could only imagine our cooler-than-a-fan father flustered and panicked at the sight and smell of flames. When that van burned down to its original silver paint, it was like a tiny bit of my childhood went to ash with it.

My father held an exalted position at the Elks Club—the Black one. He and my mother and her matching Jheri curl had an endless stream of Black friends with whose children I'd been raised. None of this popularity, or Blackness, had transferred to me. I was the one who "talked white," the one who listened to weird music, the one who was never stylish without the help of her mother.

Yet my father and I are similar, too. We're a bit quieter than people expect, though my dad is able to fake it a lot better than I can. He's able to float just above the surface of his shyness and become magnetic. My father walks into a room and the air changes. People look up from drinks and greet him. He's embraced and chatted up. It's like he brings light and people want to bask in it. Sometimes, in the most mundane of places, I find myself in the glow of it. At the gas station being asked, "You Abby's baby? Tell your daddy I said hey!" or "You remember me? Tell your dad I said to call me." I always wondered how, in the midst of such acceptance, such a glow, I never felt it extended to me. My father tells me that he never knew I felt that way. He'd assumed I always felt like I belonged. Even now it's hard to explain to him how, just because I may have been in the room, it still felt empty. But I found solace and acceptance elsewhere. I found it through music on my own terms.

The carefully numbered and initialed LP covers in our basement housed everything I saw on *Yo! MTV Raps!* Legions of emcees were at my fingertips. I could study the latest fashions and hairstyles at will. My father went record shopping weekly so things were never stale. We'd load into that turquoise van or my mother's baby blue Buick Riviera and take the highway to Akron to pick over new releases at 2 Live Music Superstore. However, I needed Greta's television to see the music in action. I had to catalog the videos to decipher what I could translate into my boring Ohio life. Just as important as the lyrics, those videos gave me glimpses into Blackness I never knew existed in real time.

I was enthralled by what I saw on Greta's screen. She and the other Black kids I longed to be were a carbon copy sheet of what MTV delivered to the airwaves. I knew my mother certainly would never let me get Salt and Pepa's asymmetrical haircuts or buy me a thick gold chain, but she would let me get British Knights sneakers and wire framed glasses and eventually the button-up plaid shirts of the West Coast. So, I sacrificed my fatness and my shyness in order to find my people. I thought as long as Greta found me redeemable there was always a chance I would make my way into the crowd.

Each day when the show ended, I'd gather my school things and make the trek from Greta's home to mine. It was a path that took me down a short block, across a set of railroad tracks, through an elementary school playground, and the crest of a hill before I could see the Y-shaped driveway of my house. Thinking of it now, it wasn't a long walk, but for a girl used to being driven it seemed like miles. But I thought nothing of it, strapped the cello to my back, and walked. The music was too important. Finding my Blackness among my own self-doubt was paramount.

It was during one of my takeovers of Greta's television I first discovered The Native Tongues crew. De La Soul's "Me, Myself, and I" video blew my mind. It was the first time I understood it was okay to be me in all my quirky, Black, Midwestern glory. It was okay to wear my Africa medallion even if I "talked white." I learned people who looked like me weren't a monolith. That video was my entry into new types of Blackness and I couldn't get enough of it. It was easy for me to imagine standing in front of the classroom like Maseo, reading from a paper extolling what made me different, or dodging direct and indirect slights about my clothes, hair, shoes, or body.

Those afternoons, there was no place I'd rather be than hunkered down in front of Greta's floor model TV. I studied the videos wondering if I too could pull off such fashion or mimic such confidence. Watching Pos, Dave, and Maseo being the odd men out was like stepping into any one of my classes back then. I was always a little aloof, quite a bit left out, and always skittish. As contrite as it may sound, those four minutes of video gave me hope it would be okay. I knew I couldn't escape my own Prof Def Beat, but I could survive him.

I said I sacrificed my fatness and my shyness for Blackness because I poured my body into a pair of pink biker shorts and an oversized flamingo t-shirt to dance beside Greta in a talent show. The stutter and stop of Sybil's "Don't Make Me Over" propelled us onto the floor of the Elks that night. And in those moments of music, I didn't care that this was years before big thighs and asses were popular. I was just a fat brown girl with buck teeth and a side ponytail who wanted to dance. So, I pulled my body through the motions of the running man and the cabbage patch with a sense of freedom I haven't recreated since.

We got second place. We lost to a group of girls called The Dolls—a group of girls dressed in all black and wearing karate shoes, dancing so hard they made the record skip. We didn't care and somewhere in my parents' house in Ohio, there is a picture of Greta and me shoulder-to-shoulder. We are holding up $12.50 each, quarters included. Our smiles are boundless. Our bangs still show the indents of pink sponge rollers. Our ponytails are ruffled.

I can't remember when I stopped going to Greta's house to watch *Yo! MTV Raps!* The show was on the decline in 1993, the year I entered Alliance High School as a freshman. By that time, my mother had given me an ultimatum to find more Black friends lest my high school years be torture. So, I did, and I spent the next four years in a patchwork friendship with a group of girls I lost contact with as soon as I left for college.

This quest to find Black friends took me to the strangest of places. I half-heartedly joined a debutante ball until I realized I wasn't as gentile and refined as was required. I could never quite get the hang of being graceful. I knew how to perch and fold like a lady, but it was more for weight distribution than elegance. I joined Junior Achievement and fell slightly in love with an Indian boy who promptly told me his family would never accept a Black girl in their home. I clung to another Black girl in our company afterwards, and looked at him from afar. And I fell in love with California. Hard.

In my very Midwestern mind, everything revolved around The Golden State. I watched shows like *Moesha, The Parkers, Hangin' with Mr. Cooper, In the House,* and *South Central* and thought I had Black California life figured out. Here's what I *thought* I knew:

- All of California is hot.

- Swap meets exist everywhere.

- Summertime in the hood is magical and deadly.

- Every good girl falls in love with a thug who needs redeeming.

- There is no middle class. You are either living large or in a terrible neighborhood.

Now, well into middle age, I have a playlist I made when I travelled to Berkeley for a writing workshop in the summer of 2018, thirty-three songs that put me into a "Cali" mood. One of those tracks, "Blowed Away" by B Rezell, is from the *Above the Rim* soundtrack. When it's on, there's not a person on this planet that can tell me that I'm not at some party with a headful of box braids, a baby tee, and a pair of platform sneakers. In my head, every man in the room is wearing Converse and oversized flannels or supple leather jackets. Everything moves in slow motion, like in the videos when someone's mid-clap and the camera crawls to a near stop, then hits regular speed a split second later. Or when the lens trains itself on the celebrity cameos and they have a small window of time to bob their head or throw their hands in the air.

But I've actually been to California twice. When I was twenty-one, I traveled first-class, on IBM's dime as a guest of an adjacent friend, and I was in San Francisco, far from the hood party of my dreams. The second time I was thirty-nine and spending thousands of dollars to workshop with writers of color just across the Bay Bridge. The closest I got to my dream party was sitting at a local bar in Oakland with a group of writers while eating tacos and drinking the best lemon drop I've ever had.

What I'd been trying to craft, after a steady stream of Black movies, television, soundtracks, and a childhood of masks, was a version of Blackness that never quite fit me or where I lived. Those friends I cobbled together during high school and I were a group of false gangstas. We took on nicknames. I was Tweety. We wore matching outfits to take group photos at a local studio. There we were, dressed in black T-shirts and jeans, trying our hardest not to smile. I failed miserably. The hint of my dimples is evident at the ends of my lips coated in Mary Kay lipstick. I'd wanted to sit in the front so my white-on-white Fila Mindbenders could be front and center. Back then, one of the highlights of my life was coming home to a new East Bay catalog. Considering I was never allowed to wear Nike like all of my peers, trying to find hot sneakers was sometimes a chore. To this day, I've never owned a pair of Jordans. It's on my Black bucket list.

If Greta was my prototype of Black girl magic, then my cousins across the tracks were some sort of coven of witches. BeBe, Chic, Tutti, Raven, Cat, Nette, and 'Ne were all the black I wanted to be. They were always freshly dressed, gold shining, confident in their words and actions. Sometimes they fought, cut the world down with the razor blades of their tongues. They had boyfriends and groups of homegirls that hung out on the concrete steps of their houses on weekends all year round. They wore the clothes and shoes off limit to me and I wanted every bit of it all. I wanted to cross the tracks and lose myself in the metropolitan houses, walk the back alley to Ralph's for bright blue popsicles, and swing a brown bag of penny candy from Miss Rachel's. I wanted to know how to make hot cuss words cool and how to turn rebellion into the norm.

Instead? I was the college girl. The white girl. The daughter of the Rockefellers, the nickname given to my two- parent, dual-income household. I was the cousin who caused an uproar with another because I was spoiled enough to override her movie choice so I could see *Spaceballs*. I was the one taken out of school for a week to go to Disney World. I was also the one too afraid to hang out or stay over because I knew I wasn't really much fun. But more than anything, I was the cousin who desperately wanted to belong and would have given up any of the trappings of her "middle-class" life to be right there beside them.

Those cousins are now mothers and grandmothers, some bearers of keloids from razor slices. Others are owners of boxer's cuts along the creases of their cheeks and corners of their eyes. All of them are still miles beyond my particular brand of cool. I watch them, during the times I am at home, as they move through the world glowing with confidence, raising daughters just the same. I look at the photos of myself standing next to them and I still feel woefully awkward and less than fly. I'm still trying to capture their footsteps or at least catch up.

When all the prior versions of Athena had run their course, I added them as more bricks in my path. They sat alongside the younger me, knees-down in front of the television watching A Tribe Called Quest. It joined the version of me who wanted to listen to R.E.M. and who had succeeded in convincing her mother to buy "white people" music for Christmas. That me was settled in with the me who listened to John Coltrane almost exclusively and dove deeply into 60s jazz. It all got muddled up with the me who just wanted to be invited out on weekends or to at least be seen in the raucous mess that was junior high and beyond. I remember sitting in Mrs. Brophy's English class listening to the other Black kids making plans for the weekend, lamenting about how they needed more people to join them. I sat there, hoping that somehow the brown of my skin would catch their eyes and they'd recognize me as one of their own. That never happened. So, I tried to catch my Blackness by proxy.

I never grew out of my shyness or my fatness and I never stopped loving hip-hop. In college, there were no more early bus stops or treks across town. Instead, I rode the Campus Loop bus in lieu of going to class some mornings and headed to the Record Exchange to buy $1 CDs. Campus was where I met my best friends, a group of Black kids from across the world who were just like me.

At Kent State University, *Yo! MTV Raps!* was replaced by live shows. My friends and I spent weekends driving between Ohio, Pennsylvania, and Washington D.C. to see The Roots, De La Soul, Wyclef, and Outkast. Chris and Mike would lip sync "Silent Treatment", using brooms as mics while sliding across the floor in their socks. Friday nights we'd pile in my silver Ford Tempo, sink into the red velour interior, and vibe out to "Aquemini". I learned Blackness came from Haiti *and* Cincinnati *and* Jamaica *and* Detroit. It had locs and baldies and relaxers. It was light and dark. It was friendships built on the staircases of Club Laga in Pittsburgh and in a sea of confetti at the Smokin' Grooves tour, my back to my boyfriend's chest as we swayed in a rain of red and pink.

It didn't take long for me to come back to Earth. Scrawled across the door of my freshman dorm room was the slur I'd thrown blows over when I was a child. *Nigger.* College quickly reminded me I was very Black despite the struggles I always had with that label. That olive-green door, a hollow metal that echoed, sounded alarms for me. How could I survive a place where I was very much a Black person when I felt like I was never really one of the tribe?

I'll tell you how. I wrapped myself in Blackness like a sash and wore it proudly even when at times it felt like I was struggling to breathe, like I was always a moment away from being exposed as the fraud I was.

By the time college graduation rolled around, just after the millennium started, I'd begun to transition my Blackness into neo-soul. I wrapped my head in yards of fabric and stopped eating meat. I travelled the country to protest against oil profits and war and eventually fell in love with the open mic. I used this new persona as another doorway into the belonging I'd sought since childhood. At times, it felt forced. Stereotypical, if you will. Like I was singing, "I'm Black, y'all! I'm Black, y'all! I'm Blacker than Black and I'm Black, y'all!" like some sort of *CB4* extra. In the Pan-African Studies department at Kent, I fell into Blackness as never before, but I didn't see it as a caricature. I thought learning to speak Kiswahili and protesting against The Man was the way to fit in. I thought my kente cloth bag made me more down.

For six years at the tail end of my twenties I grew locs. By the time I'd convinced myself bad energy required them to be cut, they flowed to the center of my back, creeping toward my hips. In those six years I cultivated them myself, never setting foot into a salon to be told how to tame them or to discuss the proper products to use. I wanted my hair to be a reflection of who I was at the time. I was a dreadlocked, vegetarian, open-mic-reading, tattooed, thrift-store-shopping, headwrap-wearing boho. I lived with my boyfriend in an apartment in a converted mansion that we'd decorated with African carvings, plants, a DJ booth, and scores of books. We hosted house parties with homemade wine where small pockets of people talked politics in the kitchen and others passed blunts on the porch. It was a life I wanted, yet still one full of places to hide.

Now, I understand I'm still chasing Greta. I'm still trying to piece together what made her tick. Not for mimic, but for understanding. I'm not sure she remembers those days I followed her off the bus. Maybe those afternoons, for her, were just another day.

For me, it was the beginning of the world. Greta had worn her Blackness with a coolness I chased after. She seemed confident in her place in the community and that was exactly what I wanted. I thought exiting the bus and stepping into her shadow would translate into invites and acceptance. It didn't. It was a foolish plan, but what happened was in the midst of all the Blackness surrounding me, I found my own. It was off kilter, rounded at the edges, but it fit. It fit like the beat of a Tribe song or the footwork of the SW1s. I carried it with me, and even though it sometimes slipped between my fingers, I protected it as best I could.

Videos aren't that important to me now, but there are other ways I catalog, other ways to be inspired, other avenues to Blackness and self-acceptance. I can find it now through scrolls of Instagram and swipes on Tinder that allow me to know that I am whole, worthy, and acceptable just as I stand. There are pitfalls with this validation, though. There are many trapdoors to collapse into and more comparisons to be made. But what's important, no matter the medium I suppose, is the act of exiting one form and entering into something new, the act of finding what fits and making it your own.

Two Turntables and a Microphone

My sophomore year at Kent State University was the year *Aquemini* dropped quietly into our lives. I say "quietly" because it was sometime after Y2K failed to end society that my friends and I rediscovered the album. *Aquemini* became a symbol of the Friday nights and weekends that began directly after class, that fall walking down into the basement of my friend Chris' new off-campus house to find the DJ whose bass had thumped through the kitchen floor.

Clad in a blue bubble coat and a tilted Yankees fitted, that DJ became a muse whose heart I eventually broke. But at the beginning of that semester, he was a shock of curls peeking from beneath a brim, hip-hop, a bridge between rural and urban. I was a baby Erykah Badu with yards of fabric circling my head and the book of poems I would pull from my satchel. I wrote while he spun, not knowing that months down the line, Atlanta would be on the horizon and for a time we'd live our version of picture-perfect hip-hop love.

By the time we cuddled together on a charter bus, traveling to see the home and works of Dr. King, he and I had moved from a tentative "who's that?" to lazy Saturday afternoons cuddled on a bottom bunk, listening to the scratch of records beginning and ending. Our nearly twelve-hour ride to Atlanta, side-by-side and thigh-to-thigh, created a bond it would take years to unravel. Those poems, some of which I started the very first time we met, were shared with him in a nameless café with food I can't remember, his leg buttressed against mine while I read from the page, afraid to look at him for fear he hated every word. He didn't, and something between us ignited, burning slowly for years—never the hot flames of passion, but instead like the embers at the tail end of a fire, low and glowing enough to keep us warm.

I want to remember the feel of the hotel mattress beneath me that night while he hovered his lips over mine, a breath away from kissing until I sent him to the vending machine for a cold drink. He'd returned with a Pepsi and news of Left Eye's death. We were late to the bus the next morning, slinking onto it while the eyes of everyone followed us to the seats awaiting us. By the time Ohio crested over the turnpike and splattered into potholes and closed factories, he and I were on the path to being one.

We were on the path to sitting in the red velour interior of my 1986 Ford Tempo with another couple of dating friends. Riding slow through the streets with 3000 and Big Boi's twang transporting us to an intergalactic city on the horizon. A city that wasn't in the middle of nowhere with us fleeing like starlings. A city that wasn't suffering from brain drain. An afro future awaited us in that music. He and I were like astronauts, always floating just above the surface. We existed in some sort of black dusk of poetry and music. We existed there until the future became the present. And like Outkast, sometimes we recorded different tracks, unmerging our sounds in order to find ourselves. Problem is there was never a reunion. Never a return to center and before we knew it, we'd parted ways and become separate entities that once were part of something great.

But back then, Saturday mornings were for his radio show, lugging milk crates of records from the car to the station and back a few hours later. An orange jigsaw puzzle he'd cull together in an old timey elevator all the way to a Black-owned station overlooking a Black city rapidly losing itself to a university. I'd call in, pretending to be Keisha from the Southside, giggling a request for the *Rapping Duke* because I knew he'd begrudgingly comply. I listened to him through the static, sat in my car for the three-hour show in my parents' driveway just to hear his voice as clear as I could get it. And later, after we moved in together, I'd meet him at home with stacks of pancakes and macerated strawberries that somehow seemed sweeter those Saturdays. Love makes everything all the richer.

Love also made us blinder. Something in me clung to him for reasons more than simply wanting him in my life. The prospect of stability, and the parallel of our still married parents, made me think that we were evenly yoked. What mattered to me was how he'd grown up just the same as me, with a mother and a father loving each other, on a daily basis, within the confines of the same home. I thought that Black love binding us on both sides was enough to hold the pieces of our relationship together. Our examples were great. It only made sense that some of what we'd known for our entire lives would transfer to us.

Even in the midst of waiting for refund checks and campus job deposits, we had a life that was our own little slice of the world. I never thought about the distance in our playfulness, how it existed in the radio waves while he was across town. Why it was so easy for me to be Keisha, a woman made up of what I thought he wanted me to be. It never occurred to me that it was easy to love from a distance, picking and choosing which bits of him I wanted or just how little of me I think he really knew. How reality saw him sleeping on the sofa as I fell into the words of another man I'd later marry.

What I knew was that we had a relationship that made sense to the world at large and to me. He loved me in the ways my father had. He was a provider. There was always food in the kitchen, utilities on, and the routine of trash days and full gas tanks. I knew where my day-to-day life stood, but I could never quite confess I was yearning for more. On those Thursdays I stood before the mic and shared my poems with a roomful of people who sometimes looked at me in awe, I never saw him. I never squinted into the brightness of the lights and saw his shadow at a table. I think that's where the fractures began.

Life became arguments about pots left soaking in the sink and trash left in the kitchen. It wasn't the feel of our backs against the glass block windows while we cooked dinner or the sticky notes and articles taped inside the cabinet doors for fun. I don't know how we existed on those fumes. It always seemed we were on a break between songs, floating in the quiet hiss of a life waiting to begin. And when we ended, again at a distance via phone, I didn't know how to look at him when I came to gather my things. When he told me I was dead to him, the record skipped, changed tracks so quickly the next song became my favorite.

In Harlem, pretending to live in the brownstone I'd rented for a romantic weekend away, he rode the rails to Queens to Fat Beats without me. I waited for him to bring back the wax that would fill the cracks between us, figuring it could be a way to make up for lost words and lost time. He called me, on a flip phone that clattered our voices between the boroughs, and told me he was lost. Everything in me wanted to race into the city to rescue him, but I found him on the other side of the door, laughing as it swung open into my fears. I was angry and when the weekend ended with us on the last train out of a snowed-in city, I wanted nothing more than to ignore him. My body would not let me.

There was still something there, something that anchored me to the life I still wasn't quite ready to let go. The lull of the train, its clacks and hisses similar to those we'd heard as we drifted to sleep back home, pulled my head to his shoulder. It felt familiar and safe even in my anger. It felt like the last few months with trouble brewing just below the surface, just beneath the smiles. I slept pressed between his body and the window, unaware of the storm outside, until both Atlanta and New York were nothing but memories we'd soon push to the backs of our lives.

Liturgy

Justin is dead.

My parents' phone number has been the same since before I was born. That's over forty years of a stable landline that will always connect. It is a way station through which messages get passed. And it's how the news of Justin's death found me. A nameless person called my parents to pass along the grief. Standing at the window of my apartment, I hear my mother relaying the message that Justin is gone and the phone is heavy in my hand, my fingers numb. My boyfriend hears me sobbing, but suddenly his arms are unable to hold me. They fall limp and useless at his sides. I am furious that all I need is someone to whisk me away from this, to shelter me from this call, but he stands there in his own shock, seeing his woman falling apart over another man. I am sure he believes taking my heart back from a ghost is impossible so he's started to give up. He's started his own disappearing. In some ways he will never become solid again.

What happens after my mother tells me my high school sweetheart is now a shell without a spirit is that I sink into the brown shag carpet and cry until I feel desiccated. I am twenty-five and living with a man who loves me and is gentle with my heart in the ways I've always wanted. Our lives are exactly what I envisioned, full of music, poetry, and friends. Justin seems like a lifetime ago, one in which things such as prom and mall dates were the entirety of the world. Before this call I cannot remember the last time I've thought of him, but now he is there in a rush of what-ifs and if-only.

Death is an intimate thing, but when you are close the grief feels thicker. People understand this mourning because it is like a hole in the world. Everything gets swallowed up for a time before the landscape adjusts itself around that absence. It's different when you've been apart for a time before the loss. You feel as if your grief is less important. Your grief is like a ghost, hard to grasp and sometimes not believed. This kind of grief is like moving through fog, hands out, seeking something familiar. It's like a warning for something you're not sure you'll ever see. It makes you find ways to filter the lost person to perfect because that is easier than remembering what actually was.

I would be remiss to tuck away the bumps in our road no matter how easy it is to sweep them to the side for the sake of memorialization. Justin was not perfect; no high school boyfriend is. I think my sadness comes from the not knowing. There is now no way to grow into what could have been. I can only take him as he was and just maybe filtering out the bad is the quickest way to sweet memory. Yet sometimes things can be too sweet. That is when the bitter is important. I will need to remember the cancelled prom plans the week before the dance or the other girl who thought he was her own. I must remember that sometimes he could be cruel in his silence until I relented to what he wanted or what he needed me to believe to be true. But before my forgetting, I only needed to survive.

After the call with my mother, I curl into a ball on the bedroom floor trying to catch my breath as my mother offers me comfort I can no longer remember. The news of Justin's death pulls me back to the Robertson Youth Center basketball court where Justin first appeared, towering over the other boys all gangly and new. It takes me back to our bodies pressed next to each other on a rumpus room floor watching Martin's *You So Crazy* on a massive TV. That call truncates the possibilities of our random reunions or the sound of his car pulling into my parents' driveway.

Justin is dead.

I don't know that only a few blocks away from my apartment, Justin's mother is shattering on a larger scale, trying to process the loss of her youngest son. It's been years since I've seen her and I have no idea just how close my apartment is to his childhood neighborhood or just how this pain stretches the blocks and shows up at our respective doorsteps. The sadness of his death is still too big to wrap around my heart, and it's sat like a stone in my belly ever since. I don't know how to digest it or how to swallow down the wails that sometimes threaten to break through. What I do, after the funeral and its trauma, is block out the memory of him to survive. Perhaps this forgetting is an ignoring of wants, needs, desires, and signs that things are never quite right. Maybe it's muscle memory to revert back to puppy love and forget this is its own type of atrophy. Maybe his death ripped the sinew of my heart and the blackness of bruise is where I've hidden.

Justin is dead.

I'm not sure I've ever really said those words aloud even if I know them to be true. When I say it for the first time, something in my brain breaks and I am back with numb fingers gripping a cordless phone. I'm back trying to clear the ringing in my ears and pull myself from the scratchy carpet. Before I know it, I am crying as if the news is fresh. But there is no glitch in my brain that makes me believe Justin is the Tupac or Elvis of Northeast Ohio. There is no hologram version of him waiting in the wings to show up in military finery. I think if I say he is dead too loudly or too often, he will appear and haunt me in ways he hasn't since he left this earth. He will haunt me because I've managed to block out the sadness by replacing it with pain I've told myself is greater, pain that belongs to me because I've lived it. I tell myself that our lives had moved on before his death. There is another woman who deserves this grief. A child who was left without a father.

He's been gone over fifteen years. He seems like a dream, a

specter of a boy I can't quite get out of my head. Justin is a ghost of a life that once was and what could have been. He haunts every bit of that time as a whisper at the edge of my memories I'm struggling to both hold onto and keep at bay. I've written about him in his casket and tried to comprehend just how his body fit inside that box, all 6'6" of him. I've written about how his eyelashes looked pressed against his cheeks. I know he is dead. I saw him with flags on either side of his casket, saw his brothers lining the front row. His obituary is paperclipped inside one of my long-forgotten journals. I know he is dead because I can remember the ache in the center of my chest as I sobbed in my car. I know because I can still feel the tension in my jaw from trying to stop myself from screaming. I know because weeks later his mother called me to thank me for the flowers.

Justin is dead.

I can't reconcile that all I have left of him is a singular photo of us, rescued from a broken keychain. That photo is packed away for those times when I need to remember his face or how his waves were always just right or how he was actually a real person who once touched my skin. That day at the mall, crammed beside each other in the photo booth, we argued about which border to choose. I won, the flowers and pastel letters far from masculine. In the photo I am not wearing my glasses because I thought I was cuter without them. So far in the future, that nearsighted haze is covering my memory of him like lichen on a tombstone. I want to be able to see his face without that picture. I don't want to dig through boxes to find its smallness among the others.

Justin is dead.

He thought he was my first kiss. I never had the heart to tell him he wasn't. Our first kiss, commemorated with a picture of me he took from the backseat, was a rainy night in the summer. I'd stretched my body around the seat to meet his tallness barely contained in the space behind me. We'd kissed with my best friend steering us down a darkened backroad toward his grandmother's home. Tupac or Biggie was storytelling in the background. Which one I can't recall. My best friend was always my wingman. Even back when she'd ridden her bike full-speed down the block to ask another boy if he liked me. And even when we lied to my aunt when borrowing her car and drove to Justin's hometown just so I could see him. I can't remember how Justin's lips felt against mine that night. I know they were not sloppy or too wet and they didn't cover my mouth like a suction cup. My high school heart tells me it was perfect.

Justin is dead.

On my twenty-first birthday, he drove through a snowstorm to campus in the tiniest car I'd ever seen to take me for a drink. We sat at a bar, his uniform dappled with snow and my eyes weary from finals, sipping fuzzy navels in silence. We'd broken up by then, but as he always said, "I'm gonna marry you one day." I wish I would have invited him to my dorm room so now I would have the memory of his body canopied above mine. I wish he would have been my first, if only for nostalgia's sake. Instead, Justin exists in pops and flashes when something triggers him to resurface. A mention of Germany or crackly phone calls that remind me of when he called from across the sea. I wish I could remember the sound of his laughter or the way his lips wrapped around my name. Sometimes I find myself Googling the circumstances of his demise in order to prove that he was real. I don't want the details of his death. I simply want to fill in the gaps of his face to make sure I am remembering him correctly.

Justin is dead.

And I'm not sure how to grieve him. I'm not sure how to make peace with everything that was left unsaid or how that death has made things better than they were. The woman I am now is not able to ignore the signs. Still, I don't know how to remember him without my throat tightening before I move down memory lane like things were always okay. I've yet to figure out how to pause and remember why we weren't together, those reasons beyond our youth and divergent paths. What I'm trying to grasp is how to temper what's left of him to grayscale, instead of the Technicolor my middle-aged revisionism has painted him. I'm failing, though, because now I've bled the color from the world to avoid feeling anything. I've reduced him to the stuff of legend, a photocopy of grief packed away inside a box, a photograph rescued from something broken.

Ready. Set. Go.

Last night, I remembered playing pitch dark hide-and-seek in a muddy field, a ruined pair of Air Max 95s, and the joy of college freshmen running fearless through the night. I am certain I will never again find that exact pair of sneakers. I've seen the blue, orange, and white colorway in stores, but something about them is never quite right. Maybe I'm holding onto a twenty-year-old memory that's fuzzy at the edges. Or maybe they are the shoes, but now they aren't as magical.

What is magical was that night, a crisp fall evening after a day of heavy rain. It was an ordinary one that shouldn't have sparked such a ripple effect, but it was a relief just to be free. Free from classes and jobs and the thickness of expectation. I was months from realizing just how many classes I could skip before grades would drop and even closer to being kicked out of honors college than I cared to realize. I was wearing those shoes, purchased with the new credit card burning a hole in my pocket, not yet aware of just how far debt could reach. All the lot of us could see were free T-shirts and $1,000 limits. We'd been naïve enough to think the campus reps knew what they were doing as they passed out free cash to starving students. Newly minted plastic in our pockets, we happily rode buses to Cleveland to stroll the aisles of Dillard's, returning to campus with bags of Tommy Hilfiger and fresh boxes of Nikes.

From the time my scholarship offer had arrived in the mailbox, I'd been afraid. It hadn't mattered just how many college brochures and letters had stacked up in the waist-high box on my sunporch.

Nor did it matter how many extracurricular activities were listed beneath my name in my senior yearbook. All that mattered was that it was for the best I hadn't accepted the chance to attend Tuskegee. It would have been too far too fast. Instead, my first taste of adulthood came not too far from the shores of Lake Erie on a campus that was a city within itself. That's where I learned just how far a meal plan could stretch, pushing until it was broken and all that remained were ramen noodles and the water fountain. And I figured out how to hide in the stairwell of an all-male dorm to avoid detection after curfew.

Freshman year was the bubble of time when I could see a friendly face across a room and cling to the person who smiled back for the next few decades just because she made me feel safe. That year saw a small band of us interlocked like puzzle pieces, afraid of facing adulthood alone. We seemed to almost buckle under the weight of still being children who were, now, expected to map out the rest of our lives.

That night, in one of the many open fields dotting the campus of Kent State University, we ran with reckless abandon, shoes squelching and sticking in the thick mud. We'd congregated in the courtyard of the freshman dorms, dressed in black, our keys and IDs slung beneath our shirts on lanyards. Trekking from the lighted pathways of Stewart Hall, we'd unplugged ourselves from the lure of Yahoo! chat rooms and the newness of an Internet we had never experienced at home. What wonder and joy was a 24/7 computer lab?

The lot of us would line the far wall of the lab four at a time, slipping on the masks of usernames and ask A/S/L? Hiding as L_boogie19, those Chocolate City chatrooms were the first places I used my words before my looks, where it didn't matter that I was always afraid to look people in the eyes. I drew in the boys with poetry on my Angelfire webpage and pored over their comments in my guestbook. Before long, I'd culled together an album of photos sent to my campus mailbox by young men who found me interesting. The distance between those men and me meant that I needn't worry about palming the pepper spray my father had slipped to me, and that my roommate would never have to unsheathe the tiny blade dangling from her neck by a pink-and-blue string. Nor would I have to worry about the pressure of an unwanted body atop mine. That was still to come.

When the tentative cross-country flirting had died down, we chose to retreat to our individual rooms to change into black T-shirts, sweatpants, and beanies. What a sight we must have been, a bevy of giggling kids marching across the field to a set of low bleachers. There is no recollection of how we chose teams or what exactly the rules were, but I do remember the sound of our laughter pealing out across the night and the chill that pressed down from above.

We sprinted and dove and rolled in a field torn up by intramural leagues, oblivious to the mud and the wetness seeping into our skin. Sometimes, we tackled each other into the juicier plots of grass and lay there backs flush against the earth, staring up into the Ohio sky. And soon, the group of us were side-by-side in the night, chests rising and breath clouding above our heads.

We rested there until oxygen pushed back into our lungs and then it was time for another sprint across the field, another squelch of shoes in the mud. We tore through the darkness until there was no more energy to pick up the heaviness of our feet or our bodies from the ground. So, we found ourselves on the low bleachers again, the steam rising from our shoulders like spirits to heaven.

We didn't know that in the near future one of us would stumble back to the dorm bruised and bloodied with the sound of racism ringing in his ears. We didn't know the way the pizza in our hands would turn tasteless as we struggled to bring our minds back to the present and believe that somewhere outside of our bubble, the real world still lurked, That night our RA couldn't save the day with stories and advice so we sat in the quad trying to find words that could reverse time. We thought maybe if we clung to each other hard enough, we could recreate the day-long water balloon fight that divided us into teams, diving into bushes, and swiping thick black paint beneath our eyes. How in the picture of the final night we were lined up like soldiers trying not to smile.

That night never came again. It was like a bubble burst, all the remaining innocence inside of us seeping out. I think, at the time, we were thankful for the isolation of the freshman dorms set back away from the heart of campus. Small World, it was called. It's gone now, torn down and sucked into a campus I no longer recognize. That isolation let us build a bond that saw us trying to hold each other together. And even if, by sophomore year, the group of us had begun to thin, something in me knew who would remain connected. By senior year we'd whittled even more and when I finally crossed the stage, only a handful of us had remained on campus striving toward our degrees. We find each other on Facebook now, sometimes between the pages of old scrapbooks, and make plans to see each as the years continue to roll by. It rarely happens. There are more children, marriages, jobs, and exhaustion between us than the miles that separate our homes. I don't think we wish for those days again. I think we simply want to remember them, maybe even long for a bit of that magic to linger in our daily lives.

But that night, save the bobbing beam of an officer's flashlight, we would have stayed there, a collection of newly minted clay statues set out to dry. In the morning there would be Sunday breakfast buffets at one of the dining halls. Monday would bring class and campus jobs. That Saturday, however, was an endless stream of thighs pressed together, shoulders bumping, the splitting of groups until two figures walked toward the dorms alone. What was left of that magic was a muddy pair of Air Max 95s, coated to the ankles, left drying next a door, and a memory twenty years later whispering *Ready. Set. Go.*

M.A.S.H.

Spouse	City	Career
Jamal	London	Writer
David	Tokyo	Lawyer
Jax	Philadelphia	Librarian
Shawn	Atlanta	Museum Curator

Cars	Kids	Home
Land Rover	Zero	City Center Loft
Jeep Cherokee	Two	Suburban Mansion
Mercedes Benz	Three	Studio Apartment
Porsche	Five	Country Cottage

Relationship
Single
Divorced
Married
It's Complicated

How to Determine Your Future:

1. Who do you want? Where do you want to be? Select four possibilities for each category of life choices. After all four slots are filled, draw a spiral in the box.

2. Count each line of the spiral until you reach the opposite of where you began—this sum is your "magic number."

3. Use your "magic number" to eliminate your choices, marking off possibilities as you progress.

4. Continue until there is only one option left under each heading.

5. Circle the final option.

6. This is your future.

Disclaimer: The life you want may not be the life you receive.

Once Upon an AOL

Fairytales tell you that someday your prince will come, but they don't do much for telling you how to keep him. There are never really any instructions on how to captivate him with song so that he's enraptured like a woodland creature. You are never told just how to gracefully glide down steps, leaving a trail of glass in your wake so that he may find you when life snaps the line. And most certainly there is never an accurate count on how many frogs you must kiss before you find him. So, a fairytale this is not. This is the story of a boy and a girl who found each other in the ether of the Internet and made love a very real thing. And I wish I could say there was a happy ending, one that shows the horizon expanding and the two of them walking off into the sunset. There isn't. At the end of this story there are two separate lives that are worlds happier because they are apart. I am not ruining anything by telling you this.

I was never quite sure how to unravel the chaos that extends over four states and across too many years. I'm afraid you'll feel that time has gone on too long, the details of this tale are no longer important and I can do nothing more than dredge up the past, but the story gets me here. It gets me to the place where I am standing on my own two feet in a life of my own design. I want to write about him, yet I can't quite make myself say his name. That name makes my tongue feel heavy. Sometimes the sight of it, on both paper and on screen, makes my stomach clench and my throat constrict. I tell myself that once I can see that combination of letters without a physical reaction, I will be healed. But all healing is relative. What I really mean is that I will not crumble or blow away like dust on opened pages.

There is a fear in being honest. For me it is crippling. At the slightest hint of feeling exposed every nerve in my body sets fire. For years my family and friends prodded me to write about my divorce. I always said it wasn't time. But with each reason as I tried to explain why I shouldn't write about that time and the rawness that was my life, the response was always the same. *You are stronger than you know. It's your story. Tell it, Athena. Tell it.* I started and stopped too many times to count. I tried telling the story as poetry. I typed out a screenplay. It was an abandoned novel. It was scraps of essays that sat unfinished in a folder titled Good Morning Heartache. I think I was trying to hold onto the story I wanted to be true.

In the time before my forced forgetting, this fairytale used to be so much easier to remember. Now? It feels like the first day of school, minus the smell of fresh supplies and new shoes. It feels like my freshman homecoming and the sloppy kiss that I never told my high school sweetheart was my first. This story makes me cower like I did in that picture, afraid my height made me too visible over my date, hunching my shoulders to shrink myself.

Trying to tell this story makes me remember the scratch and squeal of AOL, how I stumbled onto the world of poetry forums. I met him there, calling myself ColtranesMuse, not too long after I found the bravery to share my work online. All I knew of him was that he was from New Jersey, which seemed so much faster than the wildly vast boredom of Ohio. Whether on campus or tucked away in my bedroom painted the color of the Caribbean Sea, I attached myself to a computer to log on and read his words. As with so many others I'd met in chatrooms and message boards, eventually the ties between us turned slack over the miles and fiber optics. We lost each in the shifts of our lives until yet another venture into online poetry let us find each other again. We found each other in another forum, this one run by his girlfriend, and before we knew it our friendship had picked up just where it had left off.

Three years later, when I finally met him in person in the waning light of his hometown, I realized lonely is the same all over the world. The morning before, a spring day after I'd thrown my best friend's first baby shower, I'd fiddled with my luggage in a Greyhound station waiting to make my first trip to Washington D.C. It still boggles my mind my parents drove me to the station, waiting to deliver me into the hands of a couple who had previously existed as usernames and long-distance voices. The summer was breaking open into spoken word projects and website administration with him and his girlfriend. Life was unfolding into some sort of neo-soul video, full of headwraps and nag champa. The city looming at the end of a twelve-hour bus ride seemed like a place I could reinvent and shed the skin of small town shyness.

His girlfriend met me at Union Station in the nation's capital and shortly thereafter maneuvered her mint-toothpaste-colored car toward yet another highway to pick up the next passenger on our journey. Him. When I pulled myself from that car later, I came face to face with my future. This is the part of the story where the clouds part and the birds chirp just a bit louder. It's where we get to see the star-crossed lovers first lock eyes while the world fades away no matter how dangerous that may be.

Seven years after divorce and radio silence, I am unsure if his world shifted as mine did. We met in the quickening darkness that summer night. He was a tall boy dressed in all black, one pants-leg bunched around his knee, and he took wooden stairs with his boots a solid clunk echoing into the farmland. The shadow of hair blanketing the curve of his mouth made me want to kiss him, burrow into his chest. I thought he was beautiful. I thought he was mysterious and quiet in a way that made whatever he had to say important.

On the trip back to his girlfriend's home, he dwarfed the skyline in the window, blocked the spires of office buildings and monuments in the distance. From the backseat I watched their hands clasped atop the gearshift. He rubbed the back of hers, his thumb traveling the raised warmth of her veins. Their muted conversation filtered back to me and I eavesdropped on snatches of a life being built. Trading places with her, I would have driven the tiny car faster, dashing between the slower vehicles to get closer to a bed where I could tumble into his arms. She locked her eyes to the road, kept the pace steady, and the three of us jettisoned toward sinking daylight.

The next morning, after I'd fallen asleep in a chair and crashed to the parquet floor, he and I sat on a green loveseat in the quietness of morning. I felt exposed even though I was wearing white biking shorts and a blue orchestra tee shirt. His finger—an index or a middle, I can't recall—traced the outline of the crescent moon fairy tattooed on my thigh. It was an absent tracing. One that was languid and left my nerve endings on fire. My memory tells me we did not make eye contact, both of our gazes focused on the ink dotting my skin. After our marriage, we'd tattoo our anniversary upon ourselves as a promise more permanent than our rings. I should have paid attention to *Tabula Rasa*, previously etched into his forearm.

That morning, before his girlfriend stirred in the back bedroom, we spoke quietly. This is one of my favorite thoughts of him. A simple conversation a day after our internet selves became corporeal beings. We were no longer in the ether. He was real. A real man, just beyond a boy with sad, tea-colored eyes I loved. When we tried to recall that morning's conversation later, neither of us could. I like to believe it is because what we said wasn't as important as what we felt. A week later, a fraction of time into my reinvention summer, my goddaughter was born and passed all in a matter of hours and I was on the first bus back to the Buckeye State. I remember him, standing at the sliding door of Union Station, gazing at me over his shoulder before waving a weak goodbye. It would be seven years before I saw him again.

But the Internet, in its infinite pull, let me find him yet again among a sea of usernames one Thanksgiving evening five years later. He was now in Georgia as someone's husband and I was still in Ohio as someone's woman. He hadn't been to D.C. in years.

Hundreds of miles, too many memories had razed the possibilities of that first night. There were no more drives to the Capital, silent rides in the county before the city burst forth in a string of lights and traffic. Our dreams had morphed into cubicles and adult lives far from the glitter of spoken word and the hopes of what we'd planned that summer years before. The boy and the girl were now a man and a woman rebuilding a friendship while hovering over the sparks of illicit flirtation. We began again, hidden in hotel rooms across three states, cell phones, a string of work emails far away from prying eyes, and long weekends wondering what the years could have been had we known what lay dormant inside us. We remained hidden until a Tuesday in April that began with a call from my then-boyfriend, furious and demanding. He wanted me out of our shared apartment. It couldn't wait until the workday ended because I was dead to him and needed to be forgotten. Immediately. A call, across the miles from Georgia, had informed him I was the mistress of the man who had been making my day brighter for months. Now we would call it an emotional affair, one that made us feel better about the heaviness of our lives. It was something to pull us above the fray. At least for a little while.

Neither time nor distance had slowed my thoughts from that long-ago backseat nor what I felt for him when he pulled me between a bank of elevators and kissed me in a hotel during one of my grad school residencies. His marriage was ending and he was on the first leg of the drive back home. I was a detour. That Tuesday had completed the shattering of my relationship and the two of us gathered together in the shadows, waiting for the explosion, there to pick up the pieces when they finally came raining down. Both of us were afraid to admit that the flirtation we named "the spark" was actually tinder that set off the fuse. But when the pieces were gathered, we used them to cobble together a life that began with a chocolate birthday cake at the tail end of a snowstorm. Too many weekends of traversing the turnpike finally ended in a tearful request for me to stay and my rash decision to take a final paycheck and make that dream come true.

That life, among the sand that always seems to ghost over South Jersey streets, seemed too good to be true. Each morning of setting the coffee maker and cooking dinner was too idealistic to last. A twilight proposal in front of a Christmas tree and a wedding high above the city were all subplots to the real story. That life *was* too good to be true. But when we courted, between the notes of Stevie Wonder's "Golden Lady" and The Beatles' "For No One", we added dashes of J-Live's "The 4th 3rd" to make it sound like us. We didn't know the music would become our reality less than a year after I took his last name.

I remember standing in our walk-in closet while he sat on the bed, hunched over as if in pain, staring out of the loft windows into the twinkling lights of a city in the distance. It was an ordinary Thursday night in November when he said, "I cheated on you in Chicago." The world spun and for the first time I knew what people meant when they said the air was knocked out of their bodies. I doubled over against a half-wall just outside of the closet. The tears came and I couldn't hear anything else he said. When I came back to the world, I was packing an overnight bag, yelling at him not to touch me. I think he asked me to stay. It didn't seem genuine.

I do not recall driving across the Ben Franklin Bridge, paying the toll, or how I remembered how to get to a home I'd only visited once. It was nearly midnight when I arrived in front of a co-worker's home. When she found me, in a black Mercedes, I was screaming into my phone and punching the steering wheel. I couldn't feel the raised logo cutting into my knuckles. This night, Mrs. King stood next to my car in a full fur coat. She was saying, "Athena? Baby? Please unlock the door. Come into the house." Eventually, I did, but the world went black again.

Moving my things from our home before he returned one afternoon, I stalked his side of the closet, ran my fingers along the sleeves of his shirts. In a fairytale, I'd be singing a song. I'd be a twirl and bob among the hangers as the metal clinked accompaniment. But there was no song, just the beginnings of more tears and eventually the echo of sobs. Each one of his shirts smelled of a different cologne. I wondered if they smelled the same to her. Those same scents lingered on the back of his watchbands, the spot where the sweet sweat of his body mingled with the fine leather and polished metal links. There is where I wanted to roll my tongue. There, and at the crux of his shoulder, as I did when he hovered his bulk above me, my legs wrapped around his back. In the bed, I cocooned myself into his pillow to coat my memories in the smell of his head on the linen. Over time I've forgotten his voice, his smell, most of his touch.

Two mornings before our divorce, over a year after I'd filed the papers on a Christmas morning, my soon-to-be ex-husband and I shared a last talk over omelets and coffee. It had been a year of false starts, public humiliation, and private shame. I'd let myself believe that in the lingering time it took for him to sign it meant he'd been at war with himself. Maybe he had been deciding that we actually should go to counseling or just maybe he'd remembered I was a real person hanging onto the thread of his silences and what little attention he offered me.

The romantic in me, still lost in the fairytale, thought I'd step out into the cold air and he'd follow me. There would be tears he would wipe from my cheeks and he'd apologize for all that had transpired. He'd explain to me that he'd been a fool and that he wanted to make up for the lost time. In a fairytale, this is where the two of us would stand with bated breath, searching each other's faces until smiles broke between us.

"Don't think of this as an ending. It's a new beginning," he'd said back in the real world.

I believed it because I wholeheartedly wanted it to be true. We did end up in the parking lot, amid more silence and an overflow of awkwardness. There were no tears nor was there a fairytale. Years later, the only lasting memories of that morning are the clink of dishes, the sound of basketball on the TV above the counter, and a ghost of a lingering hug. I couldn't see the danger in that meeting or why it was a bad idea to let myself feel like being friends mattered. I just knew I wanted to have some part of him and this was all I was being offered. In the fairytale, this is where the chaos begins. All seems lost and our damsel is exiled into the woods or the mountains or some far-off land where she is an outsider and a stranger.

I was thirty-four when I got divorced. Thirty-four, childless, and crying my eyes out in a courtroom alone. I think the judge felt sorry for me. She and the bailiff exchanged looks and she ordered him to hand me a box of tissues. She lorded over the room, the officer lingering to her left. She was nice, I guess. As nice as someone who was overseeing the dismantling of my life could be. My divorce, nearly two years in the making, was the last on the docket for the day. It was mid-January and I'd driven from my home in Ohio to New Jersey to attend the hearing as required. I'd nearly missed the scheduled time because I couldn't find a parking spot and, if I'm honest, I was afraid to see him. Him. The him who I'd foolishly believed was my forever even though I was his second wife.

The judge had looked over the paperwork and quirked her eyebrow. She hadn't asked me if I wanted to wait for him. I figured the tears and barely recognizable words were enough to encourage her to just get on with it.

"Are you sure you don't want to ask for alimony?" she'd questioned, obviously confused.

"I don't. I just want this done."

"This is all you're asking for?" Again, she was puzzled.

I shook my head.

Fifteen minutes later, I was leaving the courtroom with two copies of the decree. When I made it back to my car, a ticket was tucked on the windshield. An expired meter. I laughed until I rolled into more tears, locked behind the doors of a gold Lexus with my perfect life falling down around me.

I think about the hurricane that hit the Eastern Seaboard in 2011 and how my ex-husband and I prepared for the storm. Bathtubs filled with water, non-perishable foods, and cars moved to higher ground was the bulk of our prep. On my way home from work that afternoon, fighting my way back toward Camden, I questioned why we weren't among the hoard leaving New Jersey and snaking across the local bridges. Apparently, we never followed the rules. Never knew how to get out of danger's way. We watched the water rising, climb its way up the trees outside of our windows until when by morning the world had sucked back its tears and we thought we were safe.

There used to be a small burning of longing beneath my collarbone. It was the need to hear a voice, to see the ellipsis of reply in a text message, anything to let me know that there was once something there. So, I read what he wrote and tried to decipher what he meant, how many cigarettes and cups of coffee it took to complete, and how far he'd come since that first summer in D.C. It was the last connection. Me as fan. Him as scribe. Me seeking clues between the lines.

I can still never quite figure out how to tell this tale. Perhaps it's in the nights after our split and how each of them found me hugging my body next to the wall, imagining it breathed and spooned like him. Or how each morning I opened my eyes and stared into that same wall hoping for a pair of tea-colored eyes to be staring back.

One April, during an ill-fated reconciliation before the end, he told me, "I miss waking up to this face." I missed waking up to his.

Where to end? In the nights that found me switching on a fan as if somehow the white noise would replace the rustle of his feet in the sheets? Only now there was no body to block the coolness and, by morning, I'd find myself burrowed, balled beneath the sheets.

I wished to wake in another life. One in which the ding of the Riverline still filtered up from the street and there was a side-eye view of the Philadelphia skyline. Or one in which the blur of our black dog was all I could see in a field of snow three feet deep, that red leash the last thread between us before tension snapped the line.

A fairytale isn't supposed to end like this, though. It's supposed to end with happiness. Sometimes there is destruction at the edge of the page or the spine of the book is broken. At the end, life may be a little singed but in the center of it all is a couple intertwined and happy. They are standing atop the mountain of all they've overcome. She is looking up into his face while he grips her chin and things fade to black on a kiss. Or at least that's the Disney version. Other fairytales are gruesome. All amputated toes, blinding thorns, and women dissipating into foam in the sea. A witch may even steal your voice.

What I know is that they are called tales for a reason. Perhaps fantasy is a better word. Fantasy leads you to believe that all you need is love and you can scale any obstacle; a gorgeous lie. This fairytale got lost somewhere between D.C. and the Internet, or perhaps along one of those quiet roads or one of the spires in the distance. This tale ends with disconnection and a lingering sigh of failure. It fades to black before the story can be completed.

Things Men Have Said to Me (Some of Which are True)

There is a light in you that needs to be protected.

I'm a righteous man. I don't want to step on toes.

I carry you with me every day.

You just don't know what it's like to have someone really care for you. Let me.

Why are you pushing me away? Trust me.

You are the closest person to me on the planet.

I love you.

You can't do nice things for women because they will think you are their boyfriend.

You're the type of girl to take home to mom, not date.

The prospect of meeting you is unattractive.

If that's how you want to carry it.

I knew about it. I just didn't care.

The difference is you want to fight for this relationship. I don't.

Maybe I like fucking her.

Your ass is too big.

I've never been satisfied.

You're a great girl. Good luck in the future.

I'm trying to make you feel bad about yourself so I don't have to feel bad about what I'm doing to you.

My dick is as hard as this remote. You wanna fuck?

My ex-wife, my dad, and my stepmother are coming over. Help me name this horror movie.

You one of those smarty arty niggas, huh?

What's your favorite kind of porn? Gangbang or DP?

Don't kill yourself. I don't want that on my shoulders.

I'd rate you a zero. You're good people, though.

Reader Insert

Reader-Insert is a type of fanfiction, almost always written in 2ⁿᵈ person point-of-view; the protagonist is always the reader, and is usually paired with one of the sexy canon characters.
—Fanlore.org

It starts with a trope: friends-to-lovers, or enemies-to-friends. One bed in a hotel room and a snowstorm outside. Maybe fake dating or a best friend makeover. Perhaps one person walks down the stairs and the rest of the world fades away and movement becomes slow motion until the two of them are kissing in the rain. Or it starts with angst, the heaviness of bitten knuckles and forlorn looks. Maybe the ugly duckling grows into herself and the crowd cheers as she accomplishes the "thing" at long last. Whatever the case, fanfiction insists the ending will be fluffy with hints of happily ever after. Or maybe the ending is just a girl, on a train, headed off to a new life. Fanfiction promises that no matter what, you can slide yourself into where you want to be and escape for just a little while.

The reader and I both know these are formulas, slots undulating enough to flex and fit around who each one of us is when we come to the story. Nothing is permanent, nor are these stories anything other than a fill-in-the-blank version of love and lust, including all stops in-between. And I've stopped at them all. The ever-pining love of Jake Sisko on a space station skirting the edge of a wormhole; the Pine Valley sweetheart of Terrance from *All My Children*; and the fic writer who just couldn't get enough of M'Baku and those frigid Jabari mountains.

For as long as I can remember, I've slipped myself into roles that don't quite fit, roles that aren't quite real. Between the roles of overachieving daughter and failed wife, defining myself was always a game of Mad Libs or M.A.S.H. Would I end up rich, poor, or middle class? Married, single, or divorced? House, apartment, or mansion? In the end, there was no real way to tell. I went where life took me. Get in where you fit in, right? But more than anything I've always felt invisible, so accurately telling the story of me starts with a disappearing act.

Invisible. It's a word that has gotten blowback from friends and family in ways I never expected. I suppose they think *they* see me. But I don't think anyone really does. At least in terms of a whole person, that is. I know they see me as a daughter, a sister, a friend, a co-worker, and an employee. Some may even see me in varying overlaps, a Venn diagram of who and what Athena is, if you will. But a whole pie chart? That whole Athena? I don't think that's happened yet and I'm not sure it will. I don't even know who I am beneath what I've constructed and the parts of myself I'm unwilling to speak about. I'm afraid, in some ways, to shout out to the world what makes me angry or happy or sad or horny. As if I can't be all of those things.

Shrinking is something I learned to do at a very young age. In most of my childhood pictures, you will find me fading into the background. Most of the time, there I am with my hands clasped in front of me, my eyes slightly downward. No matter how central I am in the photograph, I find a way to shrink. In one photo, taken at my fourth birthday party, I play second fiddle to a hipster Santa my parents hired to appear. He is slightly to the left, his beard looking as if it was comprised of cotton balls on construction paper. His glasses are huge black plastic frames. I wore the same for seven or so years.

To the right of the photo, I'm standing in a pool of mint green ruffles with my Jheri Curl slicked into a ponytail. My head, of course, is pointed to the ground and I look fidgety, like I want to be anywhere except the party thrown in my honor. It looks as if I have no right to be there. As if those gathered in the cinderblock basement to eat sheet cake and melty Neapolitan ice cream weren't gathered there to celebrate me.

There's another photo, one in which my cousin Bobby is throwing a perfect karate kick toward the camera. In it, I've managed to stand dead center and yet I'm still lost in the chaos of children around me. All of their bodies are in motion. Some of them are clinging to each other, mouths wide with laughter. My cousins' hair is wild, having escaped from beads and braids and shiny black gel. Then me. The tallest, the fattest, the shyest, the one trying to disappear despite the obvious signs it wasn't going to happen. At least physically. I'm smiling, but it doesn't quite reach my eyes. I'm sure that in my mind there was a running loop of some alternative version of myself. A me that was confident and popular, perhaps even a completely different person altogether. The photo, one I've pilfered back to Philadelphia after a visit home, was taken in my mother's kitchen—a place I should have felt wholly comfortable. It should have been a domain in which I felt completely at ease. Instead? There I am, standing in a sea of insecurity, with a fantasy in my head.

Over the years, I think I've learned why this shrinking started. I didn't, sometimes don't, want to take up too much space. This usually manifested in my fear and my shame of my large body. I wrote in a poem that *I know the way fat girls shrink/curl the mass of their bodies into a cocoon praying for big breasts and hips*. I knew I was taller, larger than most of my cousins and friends, and I wanted to fill just as much space as them, not more. When I was around eight, maybe a little younger, Chuck E. Cheese was a nightmare because of my size. I remember the excitement of the ball pit. How I wanted to sink below the surface until everyone forgot I was there. But fat kids and tall kids never really seem to be children. When the attendant told me I was too old to enter, I cried while trying to tell him my real age. He didn't believe me, and while the other children plopped their bodies into an explosion of plastic balls, I went back to my mother. She assumed I was shy. I shrank to avoid the trouble.

By the time I entered high school, I'd gained a reputation for how low my head hung. One of the football players who rode my bus always joked I would make the perfect linebacker because I knew how to keep my head down and push through. I never took this as a compliment. Instead, I always thought he was making fun of me. Besides that, I thought he was cute and the fact he was even talking to me was a miracle. He'd come down the aisle, bowlegged with eyes and face like a cat, and inside I would swoon. Somewhere in my teenage fantasies, this older boy would suddenly come to realize my beauty and forget the pouch of stomach when I sat or how I always kept my arms bent to avoid the dollop of fat at the joint of my elbow.

The closest I ever came to him seeing me were those afternoons he'd hover over the green vinyl seat and ask me why I could never quite look anyone in the eyes. He never saw beyond that and, if I'm being honest, I should have never expected him to. Forget how popular he may have been—he was athletic. Athletic with powerful calves I always noticed peeking out between his pants and his cleats. There was no way my round body should have ever registered. But I still hoped, held onto the idea that maybe one of those fluffy fics would come true and I'd end up at somebody's prom as somebody's girlfriend.

I was born into a trope, a dual-income household with parents who loved each other, a baby sister, and a pool in the backyard. I thought I'd slip directly into the exact same life and become an upwardly mobile Black wife with a husband who loved her. I went to school, got the degrees, and stayed on the straight and narrow. I abstained from casual sex and didn't do drugs. Hell, I didn't even drink until my actual 21st birthday. I wanted to be a lawyer or a *Vibe* magazine staff writer. I made my future life a reader insert of *Love Jones* with dashes of *West Side Story*. Tragic and stylish all in one.

I thought when I started telling my story in adulthood that I'd figured out all the plot holes, that there was some sort of reward at the end of the line for me. I started checking off the things I'd imagined. A foreign car. A loft with factory windows in a concierge building. A European honeymoon. A husband that fit every one of my fantasies. Life was supposed to be exactly what I wanted, a pick-and-play version of the American Dream.

It wasn't.

I had immersed into what I wanted, drawn up a battle plan for what love and happiness should be, and I'd stuck to it even when everything was falling down around me. It wasn't until I was crying alone in a divorce courtroom that I finally saw no matter how many blanks I filled in, there was never going to be a happy ending. Divorce is never pretty, but neither is trying to squeeze your healing or your story into a catch-all definition of what happens afterwards. I am not sassy, not particularly funny, and I'm decidedly unsexy, but I do know how to pretend.

I should have been aware of how his nights at the computer grew later and later. I should have noticed the way the bodies of the women he reposted to Tumblr drifted further and further from mine or how their skin was pale where mine was dark. It's cliché to say love is blind, but it's true. It's also dumb. I wonder if my ex-husband's mistress knew we were both interchangeable characters in a story that was always in flux, if she too ignored the warning signs. I wonder if she was also moving around the pieces of her life looking for just where she fit, her own slice of happiness. I wanted her to understand her love with my ex-husband was easy. It existed in short bursts of airport runs and the dusk of those first evenings when bodies are still new and giggles light the night like neon. I'd wanted to explain that when she cleaned the urine droplets from the commode and swept away the tiny, black hairs from the sink basin, she would know the irritation that tempers the high of infatuation.

But what I really wanted to ask her was if she thought I was nothing more than a character. A series of options put together in a narrative in order to drive her plot. I know reader inserts; I write them religiously. There is an ease in knowing what the story actually is and ignoring it in order to get the ending you want to be true. I know how the shuffling of a few words can change the course of action, how you can make a villain by simply stepping just outside the lines of truth and eschewing what's right for what feels good.

There are things I could not blame her for because I knew the whirlwind that came with feeling as if you are his everything. It's like getting swept up into a romance novel. Everything is warm and slow and the world melts away until it's just the two of you against what remains. It feels like you've stepped into a rom-com and you're the leading lady. I can no longer blame her for the brown hairs left in the shower or the empty box of condoms halfway tucked beneath the bed when I came home for a week's reconciliation. The reconciliation that ended because he said he'd broken *her* heart and *she* was sad.

I'm sure she could not see me beyond the brightness of their secret blossoming. I understand what it's like to write a love story, getting lost in the selfishness it takes to get through the obstacles to those brief, perfect moments. That does not mean I am not angry nor does it mean I have forgiven or forgotten. It just means I know because I've been there. I will not blame her for her tweets, her submissions to my literary journal, the blog post analyzing my writing, nor the picture posted from my home because I am tired of carrying them.

So, I couldn't blame her for thinking that I wasn't giving him all he required to feel loved or for choosing to ignore the blinding light of the diamonds on my finger. I am sure that, just as it is in the movies, she thought me the clingy wife who just couldn't let go. But I did.

What the shattering of my perfect life reminded me of was how easy it is to slip into another role. How it was possible for me to wipe the slate clean, building out a new character who was nothing like I was before. New city. New friends. New lovers. New life. And when things don't quite fit, I can still move those pieces around until I hear something click, until something locks into place for just a little while and I can add to the story. It taught me to pack away the ruins of my life from that marriage, to forget what once was because it now has been over longer than it was real.

What I finally learned, after copious false starts, is this: life isn't always canon-compliant. Alternative universes could give me the happy ending I thought I deserved. All I needed to know was where the blanks were and how to fill them in to escape what no longer served me. Fanfiction tells me that anything is possible, from the fantastic to the mundane. It reminds me that I can immerse into a world that does not appear to be mine, that a happy ending means I may need to sacrifice the life I demanded. I can be reborn after the plot turn none of us expected.

50% Off

Dark is never really dark in the city. There's always the shadow of bodies or ghosts or fears lurking in the corners of rooms. Streetlamps and cars—maybe the occasional star—give off enough light that I can never really sink into the evening. That not-so-dark is what lets me see him, even if my eyes are supposed to be closed in pleasure. I make the appropriate noises to keep him going, hoping I can latch onto something that will actually make this worth it. I press my palm against his skull and pretend to shy away from an orgasm coiling in my core, but I feel more from the wiry hairs against my skin than I do from his tongue trying to make me break and come back together again.

I spy the lick of his curls touching his ears before they fade into a crisp cut, his entire head buttressed between my thighs. There is the rise of his shoulders dipping into a wide back, and then he is legless as that odd dark eats his bottom half. He ruts for a few moments more, his tongue not finding *that* spot and then pops his head up to hover near my belly. "You like that?" he asks. "That was only 50%." There is pride in his voice, accomplishment I'm 100% sure he has not earned.

The vixen in me, named Lola from a prior relationship, wants to fist a handful of hair in each palm and tell him that unless he plows full-steam-ahead, he can leave. Lola wants me to step outside of myself and voice what I want and need in ways Athena is afraid to. She is the one who sent racy pictures with the brown curves of our shared body, capped with lace and sheer panels. The photos that made him proclaim, "My baby doesn't wear Wal-Mart lingerie!" But I win and tuck Lola back into her hiding place while he crawls up the mattress to take a space beside me.

Outside, the snow is quickly piling up. It is Valentine's Day weekend and we are snowed in, his dog and my cat getting acquainted in more ways than one. This morning he arrived on my doorstep in a jean jacket with the tiny animal shivering beneath his armpit. He told me he drove all the way from Memphis with no heat. He was not prepared for the cold of the Midwest. I warmed us with alcohol, pushing a cart up and down the aisles of the state store while he filled it with brown liquor I do not drink. We bought syrupy sweet Manischewitz and bottles of whiskey. It is way too much for two people. The fridge is fully stocked and he's made us steaks that have smoked the kitchen, the chill coming in through my opened windows.

As we sit on my white leather sofa, watching some Steve Austin strong-man reality show, he tents his body over his knees, enthralled by the action. He is short, but thick like I like 'em, and that's enough to make me forget that I tower over him. His dick is beautiful, though. He's sent me pictures of it in artful black-and-white. I'd expect nothing less from a photographer. He certainly knows its angles, so when he finally arrives I'm hoping to see it in all its glory. I'm disappointed that I get not even a hazy view of it, just 50% tongue power that makes me leave the bed and write a journal entry about how disappointed I am. But both of us know I am not bold enough to ask for more, so I nod weakly and pretend to be sated when I return. What I feel is dissatisfaction, complete and thick as the bedroom's silence, as he rolls over to sleep, his arm slung across my waist.

For two days we shack up without sex and by the time he leaves to head back to warmer Southern weather, I'm wishing for even a fraction of that tongue power because my flesh is weak and so is my heart. What I will find out nearly a year later is that his artisanal penis belongs to another woman. I'm sure she has her own private collection of gallery-quality dick pics and maybe even 75% of his power, since they dated far longer than we have even known each other.

I learn of her while comparing notes with a friend who just happens to be a common link. This friend fills in the gaps of stories I've only gotten from his mouth, 50% truth and 50% fantasy. I find out I *am* the side chick, a long-distance one but a side chick nonetheless. He listened to me speak of infidelity, told me he was approaching me with clean hands when all the while he was hiding the mess in his heart. I wish I would have known these things before I let him crawl beneath the quilts like he was burrowing to bring me to the surface. I would have clamped my legs tightly and saved the notch on my body count. I would have saved a few dollars on liquor and quality cuts of meat and let myself hide from the illusion that someone actually cared enough about me to drive 713 miles only to lie to my face about wanting to build a life. But it doesn't work out that way. I ended our weekend $300 dollars lighter and one orgasm short, wondering how I managed to pay for the pleasure of feeling nothing at all.

Butterfingers

I was standing in the aisle of a local market when I began to understand how trauma rippled. I was standing there, holding a Butterfinger in my hands, trembling. I must have been a sight, maybe a stereotype—a fat Black woman contemplating food in a public space. A woman in my 30s, afraid of a candy bar. It had been nearly a decade since I'd allowed the taste of a Butterfinger to pass my lips.

I met him on a telephone chat line, found in the back pages of a local newspaper during my final year of undergraduate school in the early 2000s. I'd been introduced to Yahoo! chat rooms and AOL instant messenger over the years I lived on campus. I worked double shifts at one of the dormitory's front desks so I had a lot of time on my hands. On the chatline, in the quiet of those empty lobbies or the darkness of my bedroom, I was popular. I seemed nice and safe, like the girl next door. *Hey! This is Athena. I'm a college student studying Sociology. I love open mics and music. Looking to meet someone new.* There were times that innocence caused my inbox to overflow with men furiously masturbating into their phones, begging for a return message or a live chat. Those grunts and slaps of skin-on-skin never interested me; I didn't know how to do anything other than blush before moving on to the next message, searching for someone to treat me like a human being. Waiting for someone to see me.

On a campus where I felt largely invisible, being deemed attractive was all I ever wanted. I hung out with my friends at frat parties, attempted to pledge a sorority, joined social clubs, and performed at open mics. All of these things terrified me and, more often than not, I ended up on the fringes of the room, quiet and nearly forgotten. So, when I was seen on that chat line, it was like the light had finally shifted to me.

He had the quintessential New York accent, so different from my flat Midwestern tones. From his first message, I was intrigued. He'd relocated from one of the boroughs and settled in a town about a half hour from campus. I'd never lived more than forty-five minutes from my hometown, and the idea of a man from a fantasy city such as New York made me feel sophisticated. After a few hours of chatting, broken into the thirty-second messages the chatline allowed, we exchanged phone numbers. I'm not sure when I decided I wanted to meet him in person, but a month or so later we'd decided he would make the trip down the highway during a weekend I wasn't working.

He arrived on campus via taxi and when he stepped out, he was nothing as he'd described. When his body unfolded from the car, the slick New Yorker I was expecting was instead a scruffy bearded man in oversized clothes. He was pigeon-toed, and with each step I could hear his soles slipping over the pavement. I couldn't bring myself to care that he had lied or demand he place himself back into the cab and make his way back up the highway. I convinced myself that the voice that first attracted me was still there, and in the moment, that was enough.

When he pinned me to the sofa, all I could focus on was the smell of Butterfingers on his breath. Then I focused on the press of the tweed sofa into my cheek, remembering that my mother had purchased it for me at an estate sale. And then I focused on his hands trying to pry apart my thighs.

Come on. Let me rub you to sleep. We both need this.

He'd come into the darkened living room and found me faced into the back of the sofa, hoping the sight of my sleeping body would dissuade him from touching me again. Earlier, when he'd come into my room and moved into my twin-sized bed, I'd forced myself to be polite lest he become violent.

I am sure his bulk pressed me into the sofa for no more than a few minutes and I can remember thinking how loudly I should scream to attract help. I couldn't move, couldn't breathe anything other than the sweetness of his breath.

Come on. I can't sleep. You can't either.

I remember holding his hands down as best I could, telling him to stop, telling him no. And then things go black. I don't remember how I moved his body from on top of mine or how I ended up locked in my bedroom. I have no recollection of calling a male friend to help me and how in an instant he was gone. Until he left me voicemails asking why we couldn't see each other again. Until he grew angry in those messages because I never picked up the phone. Until finally I graduated and that phone number became one I no longer remember.

Over the years I chastised myself for being naïve, for inviting him to stay the weekend. That second-guessing is what stopped me from telling anyone and stopped me from reporting it to the campus police. I couldn't be convinced I wouldn't be blamed. And I think part of me was concerned the carefully constructed woman I was becoming would be undone.

That day, in that market aisle ten years later, I decided I wasn't going to be afraid anymore. I'm not sure why. I can't say it was a consciously revolutionary act, even though later I'd say it was. I bought that Butterfinger and forced it down in my car before I even left the parking lot. I conquered it and let myself remember why I stopped eating them in the first place.

When I found myself in that store, shaking at the sight of the bright yellow wrapper, it was then I truly acknowledged that night. Until then, it had been a specter at the edge of my life, a shadow in the room whenever I disrobed and let a man touch me. It would take me several more years to take control of my wants and needs, casting him out and the fear that came along with him. Butterfingers are still a rarity, but I'm no longer afraid. Instead, I've learned to swallow the bitter and keep the sweetness on my tongue.

Skype Sex and the Single Girl

I try to pinpoint where this need started. There was no hot night of heavy petting that left me panting and wanting in the backseat of a boy's car. Nor was there the excited rush of losing my virginity on prom night to my high-school sweetheart. And there was certainly not the recollection of a college party that ended with slow grinding upon a bed laden with coats.

I also can't recall "The Talk" or Sex Ed, even if one of them must have happened. Maybe the idea of some boy's body trapping mine beneath his was enough to prevent me from fully tuning in. I'm also convinced that as a teenager, I could never see myself being deemed attractive enough for this to be an issue. Why worry about things that would never come to fruition? I just know that sex always seemed like a door I'd never walked through, a secret thing that even as I grew into womanhood seemed to be best left in semi-darkness. Even well into adulthood, with a man telling me that his body was mine for the taking, I always abstained until his fingers or mouth found my skin.

I wake up to a man smiling at me on the other side of a screen. I see his face and the pixelated brilliance of his teeth, the purple sheets scattered about his bed. It is a miracle my laptop has not surrendered its spot on the mattress beside me and dropped to the floor. It is doubly lucky the camera still captures my face, framing it well enough for me to see that I must have been cute in slumber. I don't know how long I have been sleeping. All I know is that something in my stomach flutters when I see him and I blush as much as a Black girl can. Tucked away in my childhood bedroom, I am a divorcée being courted from afar by a Southern gentleman who is everything I've ever wanted. If I had a checklist like Kameelah from *The Real World*, he would fill every box.

The man on the other side of my screen is, hands down, the smartest person I know. A literal genius with amazing taste in music. He is tall and beaded. Big and brown. He's a nerd with glasses who pushes my buttons just enough to keep it interesting. He's like an obtainable Winston Duke, except he's not. He's just as elusive and impossible to claim. Always out of reach and never quite real. He's also hundreds of miles away, far enough by distance and years that I'm nearly convinced I'd never want to meet him in the flesh. But he knows *my* flesh and he's learned it well over the course of the years.

When I see him, Facetime or Skype, he makes me feel like there is something waiting for me just over the horizon. All I have to do is keep walking toward it and eventually I will get there. I know this is a lie. In seven years, we have never met, never had more than a fiber optic connection that sometimes drops for months at a time. But I like him; waking up to that drawl and that smile is something I crave. He always asks me why I look at him the way I do. I can only imagine there is something in my eyes that is soft, or maybe there are other hints of admiration he picks up on through the fog of the Internet. I think I look at him that way because he's the prototype and sometimes you get attached to the thing that needs improvement no matter how rickety the construction. I'm attracted to him because I'm trying escape the crush of heartache that has pushed me back into my pre-teen bedroom and I think he's swept in like Prince Philip to wake me from this dream.

Among my friends he has a nickname, something that lets them know he is not a catfish and proves I've actually seen a person on the other side of the username. They question why neither of us has ever put our money toward a plane ticket or made any true effort to meet. It's not fear, I tell them. It's apprehension that it won't be the same in person. I don't know if I can be witty or sexy while my heart is trying to escape my chest. And really? I'm fairly convinced he doesn't want to meet me for reasons that may be the same or even vastly different. I learned to exist in the smoke and mirrors of the Internet way back when. I grew into adulthood during the days of AIM and private messages with the bustle of the chatroom moving all around me. I know that the illusion and the fantasy can be more enticing than the real thing. In cyberspace, I can be any version of myself I want with no questions asked.

When we log on, I fall into the naughty side of myself and angle my body until all the camera sees is me without a head. There are angles that make my ass look better and I know how to squeeze my upper arms against my breasts to make them perkier than they really are. It doesn't matter whether I am covered in a t-shirt or lingerie: I feel good and free, excited and a little wild. We nerdy-dirty-talk. All proper word usage and the glare of glasses on the screen. He makes me feel like I am something to be desired, so I lose myself until we are smiling into the camera again, sated and back to normal.

I know we will close our laptops and go back to our regular lives, but in those moments of pleasure I do not care. What I need from him is simply the reassurance that I am worthy of lust. I need the bite of my bottom lip between my teeth and his promises of flesh-to-flesh that will never come to fruition. I want to hear him say that he needs me. But honestly, all that *really* matters is the sound of breath rushing from his body, the tension in me coiling to breaking, and that final gaze before we say goodbye.

Karaoke

I'm a mess. I am a triumphant mess standing outside of a bar in Center City Philadelphia waiting on a Lyft. The warm night air is ruffling my shirt and moving my drunken body without much effort. There's nothing to hold onto that isn't an overflowing trash-can, so I try to steady myself out in the open. But that doesn't work and I'm swaying with my arms braced outward like fir boughs. Two of us laugh on the sidewalk, sloshed full of vodka and cranberry juice. I don't know why we are laughing other than the fact we are way drunker than we ever intended to be. The earlier drinks from the karaoke bar had worn off in the blocks we'd trekked to find another source of fun, but that is no longer a concern.

We almost passed this place, bland and dark, until the shouted offer of free drinks for the pretty girls walking by stopped us in our tracks. And now we are three double-drinks in with an old man trying to grind on two of us. Perhaps we are laughing about how he toppled from the stool before staggering over to Marisol to chat about her and the possibilities of a them. We could be chuckling about how we'd belted out Usher and Queen and The Notorious B.I.G. in a private karaoke room, passing mics between drinks.

Whatever it is, alcohol or humor, it makes us giggle until our sides hurt and we are gasping for breath. I am drunk, but I know that I like this. There is a small jolt of clarity that reminds me this is my life. One I've built and reshaped and shoulder all on my own. I think it's what I thought life would be when I moved to Philadelphia. Friends and Friday nights and laughter in a city I'd conquered. All of those things aren't true, but it's getting there.

What I have in this moment, and in this city, is a smattering of joy.

The bag of food in my hand thumps to the ground and Marisol doubles over again. She bought the last drink, the one that pushed me from tipsy to drunk. The smell of chicken, greens, and mac and cheese is enough for me to grab the plastic from the pavement and hope the platter inside isn't split wide open. I tumble into the Lyft with a raise of my hand, flopping my head back onto the seat as the car pulls off toward the expressway. The ride is quiet, save the crinkling plastic on my lap. Breeze is whipping through the windows and when I open my eyes, Boathouse Row is sliding by across still waters. It looks pretty all lit up for the night, but my vision is blurry and I just want to go home.

"You got greens in that bag?" the driver asks as we crest the final hill to my apartment building. "Smells good."

I nod and catch his eyes in the rearview mirror. The steps before me are looming as I crawl out of the car and swipe a tip into the driver's coffers. There is a part of me that wants to just sit on the concrete and let the wind sober me up a bit before I try to master the staircase. But it is late and even in this neighborhood that doesn't guarantee a drunk woman in the dark isn't prey. I fumble with the key fob, the elevator buttons, and finally stagger into the dim hallway of my apartment. I brace against the wall after I lock the door, all loose limbs and a spinning head.

I eat the platter standing half-naked, hunched over the kitchen counter. It tastes like real Black people made it and for that, I am glad. I take lazy bites and laugh to myself. In the morning, I will find my clothes scattered between the hallway and the kitchen. Shoes, pants, shirt, and purse. The group chat pings with messages of "Home!" and "Made it!" but my message doesn't come through until the next day when my eyes finally open.

The thread is full of pictures of the man I'd been eyeing all night, his stats, his job, and his name. My friends look out me for like that, knowing I am too bashful to ever approach him myself. Swain plays my wingman in my absence and sternly tells me that I better call him. We trade jabs about how old he may be. They tell me it doesn't matter. Sex is sex.

That laughter comes again as I find the remains of the platter on the counter, half-eaten and still looking tasty enough to press down the hunger starting to pull me toward the apps on my phone. This time I eat covered in a t-shirt, still hunched over the counter, scrolling notifications and messages. Saturday is bright outside. The neighborhood is quiet but awakening. Most days I try to craft the silence around me to avoid the pitfalls of sadness, but this morning I am happy for it. I listen to the robotic voice of the bus across the street cautioning that it is turning, and the family of birds that have made a home in the brickwork next to the window.

Some mornings, after a heavy rain, I find small bodies of hatchlings on the steps outside the lobby. Wind or predators have plummeted them four flights down. I try to avoid looking at them, but sometimes my eyes don't listen and the yellow flashes of their beaks stick with me. I always find myself wondering how the fall felt. If it was liberation before the crash or fear that the world was rushing up too fast. I tell myself I am thinking too deeply about birds still too young to know how to fly, but I can't stop myself from imagining that it still must have felt like freedom.

The Incredible Shrinking Woman

I know the difficulties of navigating a fat body on a plane. It starts by tucking my arms and narrowing enough to make it down the aisle while ignoring the eyes of the first-class passengers. It's an exercise in praying no one is already buckled into the end seat and hoping that just maybe the middle one is empty. So, it comes as a surprise when I find rising annoyance with the equally fat woman seated in front of me on a flight hovering somewhere over Utah. For the duration of our six hours, sharing United's ample seatbelt room but pseudo-folding-chairs, she has reclined into my knees and rocked her body into my space while she tries to make herself comfortable. I have huffed, muttered, and cursed at each jerk and press of her body because I know bright pain will shoot through my already sore legs. And I want to yell at her that *we women of size must know what it is to shrink.*

We cannot grip the back of the seat, arcing it as we escape to the tiny lavatory that makes us shuffle in, hoping we fit. And I want to scream at her about our shared tallness, how she should know how precious little room there already is and now my inches are hers. And I get tired of her flipping her hair. I am just waiting for it to break the barrier of her seat top and touch me. It doesn't, but I am still angry. And when her jacket pushes its way between the seats and caresses my kneecap, I'm not sure what to do with myself.

As we lower ourselves into California, I fight the urge to be one of those who jump up and linger in the aisle. At least there I am able to command space. My body would unfurl and I could tower, brown and proud. But as we land, the staccato of her body beats rhythm against me each time she shifts, which is often. I am risking being the angry Black woman tapping her on the shoulder and reminding her to keep her bulk to herself. "Be a respectable fat woman," I want to say.

But she is not just fat. She is also white and blond. There is privilege there that impacts our bodies in different ways. It is not the fat that separates us. It is power in the ability to say "this space is to be occupied any way I see fit." I am simply trying not to cause waves, trying to prove through my folding and tucking that I belong here. That I am not what you expect me to be. I am a good fat woman. I am reading a book of essays and I politely declined the snacks and drinks. I didn't want to be the source of a rattling pretzel bag and the crunch of salt and dough echoing.

I want to tell this fat woman about the time I cried while reading Shonda Rhimes' *The Year of Yes* on a plane toward some destination I can't remember. How when I read about the time the seatbelt wouldn't fit across her waist, I was experiencing that exact embarrassment with a cardigan across my midsection. Or the humiliation of a flight attendant making me show her my buckled belt while the cabin filled around us. Or how I went home after that trip and researched which airlines have the most room or if it was legal to bring my own seatbelt extender because I'd be too ashamed to ever ask for one in real time. How I'd resigned myself to being flung from my seat in a crash because that was better than asking for help.

I wanted to tell this fat woman about the doctor who refused to treat my knee that had popped out of place until I agreed to go to a bariatric meeting for the same hospital in which he practiced. And how I went to that meeting and then another and then another until yet another doctor made me cry. The doctor I picked next because she'd stood before our consultation group and said, "I'm not here to make you look good in a bathing suit. I'm here to make sure you're healthy." I liked her because she was honest and I didn't care about a bathing suit. I just wanted to shrink.

I wanted to rattle around the bottle of prescription weight-loss pills and tell my fellow passenger about how I had to ease onto them, fighting nausea so strong my co-workers were afraid for me. How I spent a discounted $100 every four weeks and took an equal amount of pills a day for months until I couldn't take it any longer. How I'm thinking of going back to them once more. I said none of this, just groused beneath my breath and vowed to upgrade next time I flew.

What I couldn't say to this woman, or anyone else for that matter, is that I've yet to figure out just how to exist in the world. I haven't quite figured out what version of myself I believe in the mirror. Do I believe those days when I see a beautiful woman with a body that fills out a dress like an hourglass or the version of me that has a ladder of back-fat climbing toward unattractiveness? Do I believe the me that can fit her hips easily into a train seat or the one who comes away with bruises after sitting in a stadium? Most days, I pick the fatter one because it's easier to bounce back from that low when things don't go as planned, or the clothes don't fit, or the swelling in my legs make people think losing weight would solve all of my problems.

And deep down, what I really wanted to say to this woman was that it's not actually her fault. Because it was not her who asked me, "Who's gonna want a big woman with short hair?" when I chopped it all off in college. Gave me the sage advice of "A man doesn't care how big you are as long as your stomach is flat!" Or inflicted the pain of the man I loved reminding me of my sexual unattractiveness, the largeness of my ass, and his lack of satisfaction as I stared at his equally large body. She couldn't have known any of these things that afternoon as snowy mountains gave way to rolling green hills outside the windows. So maybe I was just seeking a kindred spirit, a kind look between the seats that let me know that while her tucking and folding may have been different, she was trying to shrink, too.

And just maybe I wanted her to share a bit of her confidence.

A confidence that allowed her to spill over her seat into the spaces beside and behind her and afforded her the bravery to actually use the lavatory without fear of rising from her seat and having to buckle in again. But there is a part of me that knows my anger was rooted in fear; a fear of her constant moving calling attention to the both of us. I kept wanting her to shrink because I was doing my best to disappear and I just couldn't make my body any smaller than it already was. I thought the more she moved, the more the people around her would huff and puff as I was doing, and before we knew it, we'd be nothing more than just two fat bodies taking up the window seats and too much of the arm rests.

It would be too painful for me to try to explain to this woman the aches that last for days after my flights because once I lock my body into place, I am afraid to move. I've read too many stories of people angry at largeness creeping into the spaces they've paid for. I could never shoulder that embarrassment. Instead, I wanted to ask her how I could shed the fear of rising, of inflating to all that I am, including the reasons I am traveling. In my shrinking, I have not just shrunken my body and its presence. I've collapsed down everything I am. On that plane, and in that seat, I have made myself so invisible that the destination is no longer important. It only matters that I am not too much of anything. Fat, black, or wide.

On our final approach, with Portland gray and misted below us, she stands a final time to adjust her clothing and carry-on. Again, there is a rocking and jerking of the seat and more curses under my breath. This time I think she hears me and for a moment I swear I see a flash of blush on her cheeks. This is my final shrinking, the one that comes from being seen. This is the first time I see recognition of our shared size, but when she sits, the press of the seat is the same as it has been in the hours beforehand. I lock my muscles as we bounce onto the runway, a ritual that comes with every landing. I'm fighting the force of jet-fueled engines in order to stop my weight from invading the space of the passenger behind me.

As we deplane, I try to shake away the insecurities, tucking bits of them into the seatback pocket and leaving trails of the rest along the narrow path toward the coolness of the Oregon afternoon. I'm careful to avoid my hips brushing the seats, even if they are unoccupied. But ahead I see her with the meat of her hips swaying against the leather and I want to ask her how to reverse the shrinking and become as open as the wide blue sky.

Fat Girls Take Lovers, too

I was a twenty-eight-year-old virgin with an addiction to romance novels by the time I finally loosened my grip on a belief whose origin I never really knew. My romantic notions came true when I met *The One* and a few years after a daylight romp in a hotel room in New Jersey, I married him. I married him in full love and lust and the belief that this was my happily-ever-after. But less than a year later he was out of love, out of lust, and fully engulfed in an affair. Just like that, ten years of friendship and years of dating were nothing more than a few pictures and a drawn-out divorce. Eventually, I picked myself up and decided living in a city away from my family and friends would prove just how strong I really was.

So, in 2015, when a job opportunity in Philadelphia came my way, I convinced myself I would recreate my own Black girl version of *Sex in the City*. It didn't matter that I wasn't really sexy or bold and, for as much as I loved writing, it was not my actual career. I was far from Carrie's expensive-but-casual couture and I was moving to the city with no friends or prospects of a romantic partner, let alone several. I was, instead, a long-term federal employee who knew her way around the page a bit, so I told myself that was close enough. I was up for the adventure, no matter the jumping-off point. I packed up my life in three weeks, put the rest in storage, and drove across the Pennsylvania Turnpike to my new home.

A few months after I settled into the Mt. Airy section of the city, I received a message on a dating website from a man I'll call Mr. Philadelphia. I'd joined every single app I could think of with little luck. I'd grown tired of a few days of Black matches followed by a slew of middle-aged white men who always referred to me by the color of my skin and could never quite hide the fetish in their messages. But even worse was the absolute crickets after the newness of my profile had dimmed. Mr. Philadelphia was different. His message referenced my profile directly, and he'd actually asked me an interesting question about James Baldwin. I was intrigued. I checked out his profile before I answered and his avatar smiled back at me. Dark skin, white teeth, bald head, and a beard—just my type. We exchanged messages back and forth for a few weeks and eventually met for dinner. I let him plan the date, happy to be wooed a bit, only demanding we meet there separately so I could escape if necessary.

On a sweltering June night, I climbed out of my car in the parking lot of a Senegalese restaurant and he took my hand as I emerged. For hours, we sat in a dimly lit booth, sharing a platter of spicy fish and a bottle of white wine. Wine always makes me sleepy, slow, and warm so I drank a few glasses to calm my nerves. I bit my tongue at the heat of the dish he'd chosen and kept quiet when my water glass ran low and the waitress never returned. I was enjoying his company and wanted everything to be perfect. Complaining wasn't an option. Afterwards, we drove around the city until we ended up at an outdoor bar, debating Nas vs. Jay-Z over craft beer and vodka. We landed on opposite sides of the issue, but he was cute so I let it slide. There was no sex that night, but there would be, later.

He was the first man I'd let see my fully naked body in four years. He was the first man I'd had sex with since the afterglow of my last fuck ended in hearing displeasure at my weight and my sexual attractiveness. Mr. Philadelphia was not ashamed of my stomach or my rolls. Instead, he picked favorite parts of my body. He loved the bump of hip before my ass curved outward. Whenever we were together, his hands always found their way to that span of flesh and remained there until they found another expanse of skin on which to reside. He adored my breasts and the softness of my skin. He loved my daily scent of cherry almond lotion and lavender. He told me my smell was subtle and when he pressed himself toward me, it filled his nose. Mr. Philadelphia lusted after me and like a first love, it was all-consuming and dominated my summer. The last time I could remember feeling such a rush was those weekends I'd pressed my car toward New Jersey just to lean against the solidness of someone I'd once loved.

Now, with a phone call or a text, I'd find myself maneuvering my car down the expressway again, this time driving across the city and onto a short block. Mr. Philadelphia's home was shared with his younger sister and her ex-boyfriend in a neighborhood where I'd likely not otherwise venture alone. The house was in disrepair, a bevy of things needing fixed that had been ignored by the landlord for years. One evening, as I stumbled to the darkened bathroom, I yelped as a mouse skittered across the floor. Across town, I lived on a tree-lined street of young professionals and growing families in an apartment that was more about neighborhood than value. Mr. Philadelphia was divorced and the father of three children. I was a divorcée with no children. My salary was more than his several times over. I drove a nice car. He rode the bus. By all accounts, he wasn't supposed to be my "type" socially, but he treated me with such kindness that none of that mattered.

Some days we'd hold hands in the grocery store and buy snacks. We'd wander the aisles and he'd tell me stories of growing up in the city. Purchases in hand, we'd settle into his bed, watching television until he'd reach for me and our clothes ended up on the floor. Until I ended up on top or beneath him as he poured all of his energy into me. Until my body was contorted and flipped and flung across his shoulders, his face, or his waist. He was an enthusiastic lover, attentive and thorough. He pulled no punches when it came to making sure I orgasmed again and again and, in his unselfishness, I learned to let go.

I stopped worrying about how my best naked angle was on my back, with the slight pushing of my ribs through my skin and the arch of my behind leaving just enough room for an arm to snake through. I gave little thought to the ripple of cellulite in my thighs or the lymphedema swelling in my ankle and foot. With Mr. Philadelphia I stopped trying to hide in the darkness, searching for anything to cover my body before I rose from the bed. With him, I didn't want to sink into the shadows. I didn't have to question whether he found my body repulsive or my bashfulness a hindrance.

There were nights, after he'd pulled me to him again and again, that he laid me in the crook of his arm and asked me to read my poetry aloud. He'd stop me and tell me to slow down when the words tumbled out of my mouth in a rush of nerves. And at the end of those poems, he'd asked me to read specific lines again so he could mull over turns of phrase and praise me for what I'd created. I'd crane my neck up to look at him in the glow of my phone just see the admiration on his features. In the midst of such kindness, I could no longer hear the sirens outside or feel the sag of the old mattress or worry about whether I'd hear my car alarm in the night. Mr. Philadelphia let me transport in ways I had never experienced by just letting me be myself.

Early on, after dinner and a pitcher of drinks, we'd exited a restaurant into a yet another muggy evening in Philadelphia. Joking about my car being towed, it wasn't until a few moments later we realized it was actually true. Suddenly sober, he'd let me break down into tears in the center of the parking lot without chastising me or making fun of me. He let me cry and try calling home to my father until I came back to my senses and Mr. Philadelphia gave me my options. Take a taxi or the subway home, or stay the night with him and retrieve my car in the morning. It was our second date and the first night I slept in his bed.

I spent that night, covered in one of his t-shirts, with my date dress neatly folded on his dresser, my shoes and purse by the door to his bedroom. I woke up the next morning wrapped in his arms completely secure. Three buses and $225 later, I retrieved my car and spent the day taking Mr. Philadelphia grocery shopping for his grandmother. It was in the frozen food aisle, watching him debate over packages of peas, that I knew whatever the summer would be bring was okay with me.

For three months, between drives to Baltimore to walk the Inner Harbor and midnight water ice dates in the heart of North Philly, he reintroduced me to the idea that I wasn't a burden. He made me feel light. He made me feel like I had soft edges and there were still parts of me yet to be discovered. Mr. Philadelphia didn't sweep away my insecurities nor did he heal the trauma of my marriage. He treated me like a person and he was genuinely interested in who I was. I think he was the first person who really attempted to fully know me and what made me tick. I wasn't simply a sister or a daughter or a wife or a co-worker. I was multi-faceted, and he let me shine.

Because he let me shine, I opened myself to him and threw away my inhibitions. It was the first time I felt seductive, the first time I ever felt sexy without hiding behind a mask. Mr. Philadelphia seemed proud to be with me. He held my hand in public and even though we never entered an established relationship, I had no doubt I had a place in his life. He offered me the best of both worlds.

On a Friday night, I could be next to him listening to live jazz before heading home and tumbling into his bed. Afterwards, he'd lay there as I kissed him goodbye, off to run a 5K or explore the city on my own. We didn't expect to spend all of our waking hours together. Instead, we spent time as extensions of each other's lives. When he needed space, I knew how to give it and when I needed a bit of time to myself he knew how to accommodate that without feeling slighted or pushed aside.

I never really questioned why we never made it official. Instead, I enjoyed it for what it was. It was a summer of passion, great sex, and new memories in my newly-adopted home. It wasn't until the last days of August began to wane that the cracks in our perfect summer started to show. First was radio silence on his end and as days went by without a word, I began to suspect his infatuation with me was over. And it was. He had also been in contact with an ex-girlfriend and they'd decided to be exclusive. He let me go with the declaration I was a good catch, and he bid me good luck. The end was lackluster, considering the heat of our interactions, but that was to be expected. Connections don't thrive on passion alone. They cannot. I appreciated him for what he was and what he gave me: Mr. Philadelphia was my first real lover. Not of just my body, but of my spirit. His departure didn't hurt me, nor did the knowledge that he'd built a new blended family with his now-girlfriend.

About a year later, on a morning when I'd been feeling horrible, I saw him in my office. He was there on business and for the duration of his visit, I felt Mr. Philadelphia's stare into the back of my bright red dress. Later, my co-worker would tell me his eyes followed me everywhere. I sat at my desk smiling that afternoon, that old feeling of sexiness creeping up on me. It felt good to know that despite the absence of each other's bodies; an ember of that passion still existed. It felt good to be watched and wanted.

Three summers later we matched on the app again and that evening a text came from a number I didn't recognize. Mr. Philadelphia was trying to clean up the mess of August-Past. Even though it felt good to rebuff his offers of dates, my body and ego wanted to see him just to get a few strokes. I let my mind and heart tell me that was a slippery slope I wasn't prepared to climb nor slide down. I won't lie and hide that I added him on Facebook, scrolling through the pictures to see what his life had been in the summers since. Months later, I felt nothing more than amusement and mild annoyance when the woman he was dating added me to a Facebook message group with the women she felt were rivals. I found myself chuckling at her admission that he found playing with me funny. It was the mildest of insults among those lobbed against the others ranging from a smelly vagina to being a walking ATM. I blocked the lot of them, my mind already occupied with another man who still wasn't quite the right fit.

Despite the drama, the memories of that first summer outweighed it all. Mr. Philadelphia will forever be pitchers of margaritas in a noisy bar, paddle boats in the Baltimore Harbor, a body pressed to mine in the backseat of a cab, and an arm slung across my waist in the heat. He was the perfect beginning to my life in the city. And I know it's trite to say he was the fresh start I needed, that he helped me get my groove back, but he did. The tangle of our bodies was a knot that helped me untie what had been shackling me since the divorce. It reminded me that I could be an object of desire, not an afterthought or a partner in pity-lovemaking. Mr. Philadelphia found me funny, intelligent, and listened to me ramble about the world.

I appreciate his acceptance of our differences, how he never faulted me for my education or my career or my accomplishments in comparison to his. I appreciate him showing me his city despite some of the rough edges others would want to hide. And I'll be honest, there are nights when my bed is a little cold that I take my phone into hand and hover my finger over the screen, wanting to feel the weight of his body on mine until I break and come back together again. I never send the message because that summer has passed and we are both onto new things, new people. I'm sure my memories are worth more than anything else we could ever create now. I don't want to taint his image. Instead, I want to hold onto that fistful of heat and burn a little, slowly remembering him in the midst of this city and at the cusp of my new life.

50 Reasons to Leave Your Lover (Some of Which are Good)

He leaves pee on the underside of the toilet bowl.

You aren't his mother.

He believes you are his mother.

The sex isn't really that good, but you let him think it is.

He makes fun of you for reading romance novels.

He smokes too many cigarettes.

He doesn't want to meet your friends.

He doesn't want you to meet his friends.

All he wants is cybersex.

You're tired of being stuck in the house.

He fucks a mutual friend.

Because your father doesn't want you to be alone with him.

He is a bad kisser.

He cheats on you with a freshman.

You find a pair of hoop earrings buried in the sofa.

You find a broken fingernail in your car.

He has a secret baby.

You've never been to his house.

He's been investigated for fraud.

He's beat up a woman he met on the same dating app he met you.

He says he's a misogynist.

He cheats on you with a woman from Twitter.

Because middle school romances never last.

Because he doesn't date Black girls.

He cancels a week before senior prom.

You want to remain a virgin. He doesn't.

He sleeps on the sofa for weeks to punish you.

He doesn't support your dreams.

Because he never comes to your open mics.

Because he's angry you didn't like *Life of Pi*.

Because his medication kicks in and he doesn't need you anymore.

His ideal woman is Adele and that ain't you.

Because he thinks you're fat even though he is, too.

Because he offers to go to counseling, but still keeps seeing her on the side.

His therapist asks you what you'd do if he cheated and the room gets too quiet.

Because he lies about why his ex still posts pictures of him online.

Because the video calls always drop when the door opens.

Because he lives with his baby's mother for "convenience".

Because his baby is less than a year old.

You decide to quit ignoring the red flags.

He knows she taunts you and doesn't care.

He calls you a bitch for the world to see.

He proclaims his love for another woman before your side of the bed is cold.

He becomes a ghost and you have too much pride to find out why.

You found someone who makes you feel good even if it's wrong.

His ex adds you to a group chat with seven other women.

He's secretly dating someone else.

He proclaims you a good catch he wants to throw back.

Because his father tells you he's a taker and you have nothing left to give.

Because even though you love him you still need to have some self-respect.

Vagina, Slightly Used

"A woman can stand in the middle of the street and get dick." He says that all a woman has to do is step out of the door and there is a plethora of penis available for the taking. He makes it sound like I can sit on my stoop and watch a parade of available schlongs circle the block and happily bring one inside for a quick bit of fun. My problem, he elaborates, is that I want my heart fucked too. He's right. I don't know how to separate the two. Still, I look out of the window to see if there's something I can cherry-pick. But all I see is an idling bus and a few older men laughing on a stoop, so I return to sniffling while he tries to offer comfort.

He's made this declaration after my crying jag about the lack of sex in my life. We've done it a handful of times, some of those being really, really good. But what he doesn't do, now, is offer me consolation sex. I'll never admit it to myself, but perhaps I'm hoping he will kiss me softly and lead me to my bedroom. Maybe he will canopy his body over mine while gripping my face in his palms until I unfurl, ready and hungry beneath him. I wish for this so often that each time when he tells me he is on his way, I make sure the bed is made, the lights are low, and a candle is burning. It's all very formulaic, all ripped bodices and throbbing members, but at least the mood is set.

He tells me that he will take me to a strip club, describes how he will dress me, and how by the end of the night I will have the eyes of men upon me. He thinks all I need is a one-night-stand, sex without strings. I agree even though I know I am lying; two and a half years after this conversation, the only strip club I will have visited is in New Orleans where a dancer cleans my glasses with his penis.

The first night we met, he arrived at my apartment carrying Skinny Girl vodka in a plastic bag and he drank it with no mixer. I think it was nerves. All there'd been between us was Tumblr flirting, text messages, and phones calls on two coasts. We sat on the sofa, one that would break beneath the weight of our bodies during another afternoon. We were almost whispering even though we were alone. I can never remember the specifics of our early conversations, but this one ended with us making a path though my office, into the bathroom, and stopping at my bed. We had sex that night and it was perfect in its imperfections. It was jazz and candle-light. Too-small condoms and a cramp in my thigh.

When he kissed me, he cupped my cheeks in his hands like he actually found me fragile. I remember "The Beauty of Dissolving Portraits" swelling like a movie score somewhere in the living room, filtering through the vent, and thought I was in a dream. It was April, a time when things begin anew, rain washing away the dust and dirt of winter. This man lifted the clothing from my body and saw me in all my brokenness, saw my need to be held together, no matter the vessel. I should have been more specific in my wanting. I should have listened when a friend said, "I don't want you to get too attached to him. I'm afraid one day he won't find you shiny anymore and move on to something new." He was angry about that when I told him what she'd said, but amused enough to buy a beer koozie that still sits on my desk. *Easily distracted by shiny objects*, it says. I used to find it funny. Now I feel like I'm just another piece in a magpie's collection.

I'm thinking that first night was supposed to be *our* one-night stand. I think maybe the laughter we shared while I straddled him endeared me to him in ways he never expected. He'd whispered to me, "I want to be inside you so badly," and I let him in. Let him in as much as my body would allow and further than my heart was prepared for. I was happy that he, successful and brash, found me attractive enough to fuck and interesting enough to stay the night. So, I didn't ask questions or demand anything he wasn't willing to give. I was simply happy for the warmth of a body next to me and the notifications on my phone.

When I lost my virginity at twenty-eight, I'd finally convinced myself that sex wasn't as sacred as I'd made it out to be. I'd been either saving myself for marriage or waiting on a seemingly perfect man. I expected sex to be some sort of spiritual connection, full of pomp and circumstance. But I'd absorbed a steady stream of Danielle Steele books and Arabesque romance novels among the stacks of Rodman Public Library, so things were kind of skewed from the beginning. Yet, because there was a part of me that wanted to be objectified, I accepted what he offered. It pains me to admit that. It hurts to think that I exited the wreckage of my divorce wanting not to be loved, but possessed in ways I'd never experienced.

However, those romance novels never left me even as I stocked my nightstand with Magnum condoms and KY Jelly. I was still fighting the vestiges of Francis Ray's Grayson family series, wanting someone to cherish me like Luke and his brothers did their wives. So even if I told myself I was okay with the sling of my legs over his shoulders or the smack of his heavy hand against my ass, I cherished the time he arrived with orange juice and meds when I was sick. I wanted more of him cooking in my kitchen while he shooed me away from the smells, and I wanted the tiny intimacy of the grip of his fingers on my toes as we watched Netflix. I did my best to ignore all he never offered me, like the keys to the inner circle of his life.

It's because I'd felt so invisible my entire existence that I gathered greedily what was laid out before me. I've always felt like my being deemed desirable by a man was a fluke. I can remember my door swinging open as, on the other side, he drank in my freshly weaved hair and said, "You *are* pretty today." And I couldn't help but to wonder if he only believed this to be true because I'd said it first over the phone before his arrival. Because I can't quite remember him saying it before. He said I was a good person. Said I was talented. Never pretty. Never beautiful. Never sexy. Except that one time in bed when I'd said I wasn't and he'd made me crawl toward his naked frame and praised just how pretty I was as I gave him head. And like that sofa, the bed broke, too.

One December, on my birthday, I woke up to a smoke alarm caused by thirty-nine candles on a cake. I thought, "Hold on just a little while longer, he's just afraid to feel anything." I should have told myself I was feeling too much, expecting things he was not willing to give and had never intended to. And at dinner, high above Philadelphia, we scraped utensils across plates and watched the city glitter below us. It had been seven years since I'd taken that elevator up thirty-seven floors to overlook the city. Back then, I'd been in a private room at the back of the restaurant getting married to a man who'd later say that he felt like a bomb was about to explode, that he knew of our demise.

After dessert, he and I walked in the cold December air a few blocks back to the hotel and I wanted him to hold my hand because I wanted to pretend that he actually belonged to me. I waited for his arm to snake around my shoulder or his lips to press to my forehead, those intimacies that would clue me in on whether he actually felt anything. I thought they would mean somewhere in the jumble of mixed signals he just didn't know how to say what he felt. It never occurred to me I was giving off mixed signals, too. Because I never expressly told him what I needed. Instead? I hemmed and hawed and made sweeping statements about not being seen, not being wanted. It was his gaze to which I was referring. I kept a buffer between what I wanted and what I said, so afraid of rejection and loneliness that I blinded myself to the obvious. He didn't want me.

For those hours at dinner I let myself remember the careful decorations I'd walked into that morning after we'd waved the smoke from the air and finally left my bed. How the dining room table had been set for breakfast and gifts were wrapped beneath banners and balloons. I sank into the knowledge that a few blocks away from the restaurant there was a yet another bed awaiting us. And lastly, when he left me, hoping he'd reach for me, alone in that bed sometime between night and morning, I remembered he was not and could never be mine. He'd always proclaimed, "I'm not beholden to anyone." I should have listened, should have never tried to sweep him into my own personal fanfiction or make him the object of a desire that would never be returned.

When he disappeared it broke my heart. Our daily conversations dwindled down to nothing. The following birthday, instead of a blaze of well wishes, there was a voice text and a promise of a gift. He left me with a bevy of secrets and shame but no explanation of just what went wrong. I kept remembering his declaration that a man fucks what he wants and if he doesn't like it he will never fuck again. I sat in that confusion, wondering to where all those magical dicks on my block had disappeared. The one I wanted had been sitting next to me, but it may as well have been locked behind glass, only to break in emergencies. My need to be a body before a heart didn't rise to the occasion. I couldn't quite figure how to tamp down the spate of tears each time he repeated that women had it much easier than men, that all I had to do was walk out into the open and catch what was dangling right in front of my eyes.

A Love Supreme

It's an odd quiet, the life of a pre-divorcee. There is the sizzle of polenta in a skillet after work on a Wednesday, but no more gurgling coffeemaker after the buttons have been pressed to keep a lover awake. And yet, between the strangled sobs bouncing off the bathroom tiles and the way *A Love Supreme* echoes against hardwood floors, landing on the softness of a slate-blue sofa, the quietness isn't really quietness at all. It's the chaotic stillness of a woman who no longer knows what to do with her hands. What to do with the leftovers of a love that withered like basil on a windowsill?

Quiet is relative, no matter the television volume, the chirps and blips of gadgets, or the purr of an engine. Quiet is in the heart. It is the dropping of pronouns. No longer *we* or *us*. Quiet makes the questions boomerang.

She worries how she must appear to her new neighbors. So little furniture, out-of-state license plates, a life that starts at sunup and ends with the extinguishing of the porch light. Normal life sounds are reduced to the faint strains of jazz filtering skyward through vents and the single set of footsteps moving back and forth from living room to bedroom and back. No pizza delivery, no visits, no noise. Just the nearly silent ins-and-outs of a woman with tired eyes and a mass of keys announcing each arrival and departure.

This stillness is massive. It hovers and settles, retreats and returns. Almost breathing. Certainly fluid, viscous. Too thick to remedy with Girls' Nights Out or spa days. There are no clubs and drunken text messages that can fill the void with his voice. She wants to drive her car into traffic and stop the quiet, once and for all. But she isn't selfish. Then she thinks about the bottle of store-brand sleeping capsules, the only way she's been able to sleep during the last two months and eighteen days. Warned against addiction, she lies to the world and claims she sleeps without them, yet each night the blue gel pill makes its way from the dresser-top down her throat. There are fifty-seven in the bottle. Enough to slow her breathing until cessation, leaving her presentable for a funeral. She fills the yellow pitcher halfway with water and palms the bottle. This small rattle of death is the last sound until the stillness lifts.

It's an odd quiet. The life of a pre-divorcee who is more afraid of the darkness than she is of the quiet. It is the sound of hammers hanging drapes and the rearranging of furniture. It is finally reaching out. To an ex. To an old friend. To a father. To the world, bit by bit. It is the ability to make plans that extend past each workday, beyond the hours between employment and sleep.

Quiet is relative, no matter the echoes through the emptiness of a domestic life being rebuilt, the single dinners. Quiet is in the heart. It is the return of pronouns. Now *I* and *me*. Quiet makes the questions boomerang. Makes them roll off the skin like oil.

Lakeshore

Somewhere in a man's memory in Chicago, I am nothing more than failed head in a hotel room. I can picture the aftermath: him sliding the bulk of his body into his car after the valet brought it 'round for him. I can see him disappearing into the streets of the city while I am left behind, shaky and trying to catch my breath. He is escaping his actions, Polo'd down from the width of his shoulders to the bottom of his feet. But I am there, balanced on the edge of a bed in the W Lakeshore, a bowl of congee and a crème brûlée warming on the desk, the condensation of a Coke sliding down my palm, my hand trembling from my gulps. I am trying to stop my skin from burning. The back of my neck still hums from the press of his hand. I told him, "I can't. I'm on my period."

He is unfazed, standing and pushing his pelvis toward my face. That hand, heavy not in weight but intention, is barely a whisper against my body, but I know the pressure of him willing my head forward toward his unbuckled jeans. The printed rim of his boxer briefs, Polo too, peeks out at me like a black hole threatening to swallow me entirely. He doesn't say anything aloud, but his body is screaming for pleasure in ways I am unwilling, or able, to provide.

I am supposed to be in Chicago only to visit the Field Museum, not to meet up with a man I've only known through Tumblr. When I drove the hours between Ohio and Illinois, I daydreamed about uncovered bones and new memories of old things. I thought of water lapping against shores and room service—anything to forget that in this city is where my husband's affair began. Instead of sticking to my plan, I make him my first stop after an impromptu DM and push the museum to the next day. I invite him to my hotel room that overlooks the lake and the pier jutting from its shore, telling myself I want to put a face to a name. But it is hard to separate my intentions from his desires and even harder to erase the hum of his touch from my skin. After he leaves, I scrub myself clean in the hotel bathtub, gliding the white bar of soap across the parts of me he's touched until I feel too slick to safely exit. I sit there wondering when my body will feel like my own, when I will stop doling it out for scraps of warmth that are soon snatched and shattered like amber before me.

I don't sleep that night, but the following morning, I find my way through the Middle Passage exhibit, pitching my body through the dark. In the haziness of the mock ship, I am frightened by the ghostly shadows of slaves stenciled into the walls. I squint trying to find them more solid then memory. I feel sick to my stomach. There is something about the space that sets my heart pounding and makes me dizzy. I want to escape these ghosts, escape the eerie silence changed only by the creak of my sneakers against wooden planks. But I can only hold onto the fact I am, steadily, moving forward.

I know there is another patron several steps behind me and he is just as dizzy, if his footsteps are any indication. I hear the drunken pattern as he tries to find the wall and I know he is looking for any sliver of light that will guide him out of this darkness. I adjust my eyes, learning how to see through a pitch black that seems endless. I move forward toward sounds, maybe a human voice or two. I do not want him to catch up to me. I am overwhelmed enough without the scent of his cologne in my nostrils or his shoulder brushing mine, but I hear him and the space is getting smaller and smaller. My steps are even more unsure. I want to buckle, to collapse down into the nearest corner until he passes and my breath evens. I feel ashamed.

Ashamed because he is not the one who is still looming in the corners of my hotel room and my now further-tarnished memories of this city. Ashamed of my fear because this museumgoer's nearness is nothing. Or I tell myself it is. I say, "No man has ever raped you. Assault doesn't count." I rationalize and rank penetration higher than unwanted touching. I convince myself that things could always be worse. I say to myself, "At least you weren't washing the taste of him out of your mouth or the blood from your thighs."

I feel the fear at my back like wind, and I slow enough to let the man pass. I pretend to be interested, maybe enraptured, by the eyes staring out from all around me. I stay there, pushing and pulling shaky breaths until I am alone in the dark. I want to press my palm against the wall, to steady and connect, but this is a museum and even in my fear I am respectful. But I tuck that fear inside and concentrate on putting one foot in front of the other, knowing that in the morning this will be a memory and Chicago will only be a skyline in the rearview mirror. I keep moving toward the light at the end of the tunnel, emerging at last, stunned in place by a "SOLD" sign standing as a welcome and a warning.

An Imprint Instead of a Flash

Route 62, straddled between Canton and Alliance, Ohio, can barely be called a highway. It's a two-lane passage with stoplights, farms, and the occasional cow, punctuated with swaying rows of corn, a whooshing synced with the sound of tires on the road and the echoes of the Stark County Jail. Route 62 is where I chose to die.

It's where I drove my tiny sports car toward the rear end of a tractor-trailer on my way home from work. I'd been tired for months, telling you, my dear mother, how difficult it was to rise from bed each morning pretending that I didn't want to simply disappear. I think you believed "tired" meant I was weary of my divorce proceedings and the loss of my life in New Jersey. So when I arrived home, battered and dark-eyed, you'd done as expected. You cooked and coddled and cooed. I was still tired, but I smiled and pretended everything was okay. I learned to wear masks.

I didn't confide further in you; knew you'd never understand what drove me to that moment with the staccato of the brake lights as the truck ahead of me slowed to a stop. I locked my arms and gripped the steering wheel, almost pressing my body through the bucket seat as I smashed the pedal to the floor, accelerating.

Route 62 is the middle of nowhere. Far enough from the city hospitals that a person could die en route. I think, now, that was the plan, except there never really was a plan. I think I'd just run out of energy and, in that moment, that final act was all I could muster. I hadn't thought about how you'd react to what remained of my body or how you'd blame yourself for not understanding what tired meant or worrying about how you'd afford to bury your oldest daughter.

So I stopped. I decided if I needed to die, I'd allow you the dignity of an open casket. I thought that would be my gift to you; no further need to bring your daughter out of a tailspin. At your father's funeral, my own father had leaned over and said he'd go insane if anything were to happen to me. When my car barreled toward the back of that rig, I did not remember that. I'd only wanted to be selfish, believing that if I ceased to exist, the world wouldn't blink.

But for you, it would have cracked open and spilled into darkness. I was tired, beaten down by months of infidelity and the jagged words of a man doing anything to break my spirit. What could it matter if I finished off my body? It never occurred to me just how many times in your life you'd driven that road; how many more you'd have to drive it during your lifetime.

Route 62 connected you to your hometown, twenty-one miles down a flat expanse of roadway colliding into a Wal-Mart and Triple 7 slot houses. It was the thread connecting you to your mother, sisters, brothers, and the rest of our family. I did not think of them. I did not think of my sister and how her life would have been cleaved. It was selfish to think life would have been better. Life would have been different.

My life did not flash before me. Instead, that intersection imprinted. The white farmhouse and barn to the left, the cornfields on the right, the movement of the traffic signal in the breeze. Three years after that day, I'd drive through that intersection time and again with you, never revealing why I always grew silent. It took me years to confess just how close I'd come to leaving every bit of myself behind.

Route 62 branches off like a cross every few miles, pulling residents deeper into farmlands which give way to a city center celebrating football and the violent concussion of bodies slamming together. It pushes past memories: the DMV where I failed my first driving test, the car tapping the orange cone ever so slightly; the small brick apartment houses where my grandmother still lives after her husband's death; the Church's Chicken where you and my father courted while you worked; and eventually the rising steps of Mt. Nebo United Holy Church, where the sound of God spills beyond the altar.

When I aimed my car toward the metal edge of that semi, I did not think of those memories. Instead, I remembered my failed marriage, the ache in the center of my chest that made it hard to breathe most days, the breaking down of what I'd known about myself. Without my roles, as wife-sister-daughter-friend, I didn't know who I was. All of me was wrapped up in being all things to all people. Strip that away and I thought there was nothing left.

How could I move forward when my life was a skeleton of what it was? There was nothing to flesh out the quiet times. Nothing to stop me from retreating so far into my head that I was blinded to all that is good. That is when I drove toward the end of my life on a two-lane highway, waiting for the light seeping into my closed lids to finally give way to nothing, but I was too afraid to finish the deed because my last act on earth would be the opposite of how I'd lived. In those moments, my life was not my own. It belonged to those who were to be left behind. I had to remember how the scent of my death would linger in the places that made their lives move. A highway. A bedroom. A car. A place connected to happier times. It was then I knew I could not be self.

When you and my father read another account of that day, he calls me. He tells me he knew "tired" was more than just weariness. But he didn't know that it was actually apathy that had sunken into my bones. He did not know how long I'd abused my body by not eating or sleeping. How on that day I'd made it through work with burning eyes, dizzy and on the verge of collapse. Neither he nor you knew how my hair fell in soft drifts in my bathroom each morning, looking into a mirror where I'd scrawled affirmations to buoy myself. Nor did you know how underneath my clothes, my body was a canvas of bruises. Night terrors pitched me into screaming every evening, or sleep paralysis strapped me to the bed in the quiet of my empty apartment. That day, I simply wanted it to end. I wanted to cease feeling anything.

I began to believe that I was disposable, invisible, that there was no up, like I was screaming into a void. My voice was sucked up and spit back into a world of people serving platitudes that did nothing more than highlight just how expansive that void was. There was nothing you could have said to put me back together.

Eighteen miles after I slammed my car to a stop behind that truck, I exited Route 62 into my hometown. When I pulled into the driveway of your house, the gravel crunching beneath the tires, I took time to gather myself before entering. I had learned to wear masks. I knew to make small talk about the office and my plans for the evening. When I returned to my own home a few blocks away, I did as I had each night for months. I stripped away the world before curling into a ball atop the mattress, the glow of a laptop next to my face. I was convinced the opportunity had passed and I'd have to find another way to die. It would present itself months later in the form of a bottle of sleeping pills. A much cleaner death. One that would allow a bit of respect for you.

The sun rose the morning after the truck, forcing me onto Route 62 again. In the twilight of day beginning, there were no trucks on the horizon, just other cars. Cars with people who had things to live for. I wasn't selfish enough to use them as my tools of destruction. I went through the motions of living again. I did it each morning, passing that intersection and never again coming across the perfect opportunity of death. And after those sleeping pills that cemented me to the edge of my bed for hours, I had to figure out a way to live. There is no redemptive story I can tell you. I can tell you that I am still here.

Depression Is a Pair of Panties

In the blued dark of early city morning, I riffle through the third drawer of my dresser. *The* drawer, the one that houses all of the panties I hate to wear. It sticks sometimes and there is the scratchy creaking of wood on wood. The drawer opens, finally, and a rush of fabric pushes forth, scraps of it thudding quietly to the floor. I spend way too much time sifting through them. I know there is a scant thirty minutes between the time my eyes open and when I have to be on the road to my office. Panty choice takes up five. It all depends on a number of factors: most importantly, I need to know what jeans I am wearing and where my shirt will fall.

These third drawer panties are the boy shorts too tight on the ass and thighs and the thongs that seemed like the correct purchase when I wanted to feel good about myself. The lot of them are uncomfortable or not practical or maybe even a little raggedy. A handful of them are meant for someone special who doesn't yet exist, but the deal was too good to pass up. Some people would look at this drawer and say some of them are period panties, but they aren't. Rather, they are clean undergarments for when weeks have gone by and I am finally down to the items that will draw me out of my funk and force me to function. They are like jeans that are too big on the waist so I spend the day shimmying and pulling them up. Like socks that slouch into my shoes and make the bottom of my feet hurt. Maybe a hoodie splashed with bleach or a pair of sleep shorts rubbed raw in the thighs.

After work when the city is turning to blue haze again, I find myself scrolling plus-sized websites for new panties. I tell myself that one way out of this low is to empty out the drawers and order everything new. Six months ago, I did the same with socks. So, I order two Fenty bras, one icy-blue lace that when it arrives should make me feel sexy. The other is practical and black. But I'm not sure what kind of panties to buy. I need to be realistic. I know no one will see them, so comfort is more important than sex appeal. *Be serious*, I tell myself as I scroll Target, Wal-Mart, and ASOS. I finally convince myself to find a middle ground—cotton with a little embellishment. A little dangerous and a lot pulled-together. Kinda like me.

My most recent work review says, "Very dependable. Willing to adapt to changes in schedule. Kind and friendly to co-workers." This morning, I am driving toward my cubicle with a gas tank that is blinking near empty. My inspection sticker is missing and my identification is expired. My sick leave is stockpiling because I never take it and it's a fairly well-known fact that before the clock flips to 7:00 AM I will already be at my desk logged on and ready to serve.

At home, the dishwasher has completed its cycle. The dishes are clean, but they will sit there until something forces me to store them in their proper places. That "something" is not being able to use my favorite fork. I need the weight of it in my hand before food can touch my tongue. I know I am in a cycle of my own that sees me appearing pulled together to the world at large, but slowly dissolving away on the inside. It's a dangerous game, *how far can I ignore the responsibilities of life before something falls apart?*

Each morning as my work computer cycles itself to life and I enter the proper codes, I place a tiny peach pill next to the keyboard. It controls my blood pressure, makes the whooshing in my ears dull to nothing. I swallow the pill with a swish of Coke because coffee is the last thing I want to consume. But I am tired and frequently remove my glasses to rub my eyes. I wait for the auto-start programs to populate the screen and try to settle my stomach. I feel sick each morning, but I am at work without fail. Each night I fall asleep via melatonin and a white noise machine. I try to drown out my thoughts and remember that I cannot fix nor save the world. I try to remind myself that I am worthy of rest and care even if the only source of it seems to be me. A friend tells me that I'm always looking ahead, that I never enjoy the little moments. What he doesn't understand is that I know the little moments all too well. Those are where I get lost, the places I try to escape before I lose myself in the sadness.

I know that I need to go grocery shopping because GrubHub gets way too much of my money and it's not healthy to eat out as much as I do. There is a store just down the block, so close I can walk to it with very little effort. It is open twenty-four hours, too. But it is not a simple task to gather the bags and make my way down the aisles pulling items from the shelves for meals I know I will never make. That produce will eventually rot and be thrown into the trash can that it will take all my energy to carry to the dumpster. So I cave to the little red heart that tells me which of the restaurants are my go-to and I order the same food without fail.

Depression and its twin, anxiety, are not beautiful for me. I have never perched wistfully while gazing out of a window nor have I made myself into a blanket burrito in the center of my bed. Instead, I sometimes cry on my sofa when a commercial hits a little close to home, or randomly in the bathroom for reasons I can't discern. But I'm good at hiding those cracks, or at least I think I am. My friend tells me the first time she met me I looked dark. "You didn't look bad. Just tired," she said. I was fine with that. At least I was alive, unmaimed, and functioning well enough to travel to Boston for a conference. I had the wherewithal to stand at a podium in a room full of people and sound like I knew what the hell I was talking about. She tells me now that she is proud of me, that she can see the light I've gathered over the years.

I make a throwaway post on Tumblr one night about how being a high-functioning depressed person is terrible because people assume you are okay. They see you going through the motions, even laughing and smiling, and think all is right with the world. A few months ago, someone I've known nearly my entire life jabbed at me that she saw me going to dinner and hanging out with friends while she just worked and took care of her kids. I wanted to shout at her that she had no clue just how many invitations I'd declined or what I would give to come home to children or a spouse. She doesn't, maybe will never, care that there are days when it takes all I have to just rise from bed. She seems to believe that a few pictures on Facebook means I am living my best life. What it really means is I know how to crop, copy, and paste.

My Tumblr post gains a little traction and before long several hundred people have re-blogged it. I feel seen, even in the chaos of the Internet. I am glad to know that someone else understands what it's like to be held together with sheer will and fear of disappointing the world. Those people behind the usernames know what it's like to be the rock.

When the panties finally arrive, they are bundled into a non-descript white envelope crammed inside my mailbox. I scatter them across my bed in all their purple, blue, pink, and pastel glory. They are boring. So boring that I wonder if I was in my right mind when I clicked the purchase button. Maybe I'd spent so much time trying to find the perfect compromise that I accidently ordered the most basic, brief-cut panties known to womankind. I stuff them into the "okay" panty drawer anyway. I know in the darkness of morning I will feel their softness against my fingers and know they serve their purpose until I find myself in a new cycle, favoring a particular set of underwear so much that I'd rather do laundry more often than be without the pair of them in the drawer. It's a crutch, I know, but it helps me feel normal. I start to take this approach in other areas of my life.

I load the dishwasher and run it for the glasses, plates, and utensils, but leave the pots to soak in the sink. I force myself to put the trash bag next to the door so that I have no choice but to take it down the elevator with me. I become adept at hyping myself up just enough to buy one bag of groceries, stopping at the store before I go home from work. I clean one room of my apartment at a time so things aren't too overwhelming. And I make lists, paper and digital, to remind me of when bills need to be paid and the things I have to do. It works, but there are still the commercials that remind me of what I am missing. I'm not sure why these things trigger me, but they do.

The commercials tell me I should be happy. They say that I should be having morning sex and taking Plan B if something slips out or into a place it shouldn't be. They show me that all I need is real cheese and a luxury car, maybe even a mortgage that will get me into the perfect neighborhood for the children I don't have. And the commercials want me to wear the right jeans with the right shoes to go to the right places on a Friday night. Sometimes I look at my life and know I can have all of those things, to some degree. They are within my grasp, both monetarily and socially. But the commercials do not account for the plans I make and cancel because anxiety has me worried about where I will park, who will be there, and if I will look out of place. They do not take into account just how difficult it can be to leave my apartment and how sometimes the sounds of human voices grate on my nerves so badly even my television stays off for days at a time.

Fresh panties bound out of the drawer each morning. The only true decision I have to make is which color suits my mood. I slide them on and stand before the mirror in my bedroom to inspect myself before slipping my clothes over them and setting my mask for the world. I check how many pairs are left between the two trays, calculate just how much farther I can push it before I'm back to scraping the bottom for bits of scratchy lace or low-rise nightmares. I spy the jumble of jeans on my bedside chair, the multiple pairs of the same dark-wash skinnies, and the battered Converse tumbled beside them. This shows me there are yet more layers to replace. There is more armor to solder, more threadbare places I am hiding behind that need stitching and repair.

Acknowledgments

A version of "Ready. Set. Go." appears as "Squelch" in *The Great Lakes Review* (September 26, 2017)

A version of "Butterfingers" appears as "Butterfingers are Revolutionary" in *So To Speak Journal*, #metoo blog (2018)

"A Love Supreme" appears as "A Love Supreme: The Life of a Pre-Divorcee" in *For Harriet* (March 13, 2012)

"An Imprint Instead of a Flash" appears in *snapdragon: a journal of art & healing* (Winter 2018, Issue 4.4)

"The Incredible Shrinking Woman" appears in *GAY Magazine*, 05/01/2019

Gratitudes

I can only offer infinite thanks to my parents, Albert and Sharon Dixon, for the sacrifices and support you've given me my entire life. Even if you didn't understand where my path was leading, you let me experiment, fail, and rise without wavering.

To my sister Evona Bowman. You are one of the most amazing people on this planet. You are kind beyond words, creative beyond measure, and I'm lucky to call you my Kid Sister. Thank you for picking me up when I am down, for singing my praises when my voice cracks, and for each and every bit of laughter.

All the thanks to The Original Shenanigans Squad: Marisol Serrano, Kymberli Morrell, Ashi Lindsay-Washington, Jennifer Swain, Phorlie Tsen, and Rebecca Lugo. You ladies are my absolute best friends. You've helped me make Philadelphia a home. Some of my greatest adventures have been with you and I can't wait to see what is on the horizon.

To Angie Chatman. My right-hand woman. My surrogate big sister. My voice of reason and the stern hand I sometimes need. Thank you for reminding me of who I am when I forget and for dragging me out of the doldrums with love and a healthy dose of side eye.

The ladies of *Linden Avenue Literary Journal*. Thank you for keeping my dream alive and bringing it the breath it needs.

To my readers Cija A. Jefferson, Jen Soong, and Lara Lillibridge. Thank you for helping me take a bagful of glass and press it into the reflection I wanted, and needed, to see. Thank you for reminding me I have a voice and it needed to be heard. Your writing and your stories inspire me.

My classmates at Tin House Winter Workshop (2019), Callaloo (Oxford 2017), and V.O.N.A (2018), but especially my Page 71 ladies. Thank you for seeing some of these essays in their fledgling forms and giving them the careful eyes, tough love, and respect they deserved. I wouldn't have finished this book without your input.

To the Black Panther Fan Fiction Community. Thank you all for helping me become more comfortable with prose, for being enthusiastic about my stories, and for showing me that a writing community comes in all forms. Once the world learns of your talents it will never be the same. You ladies are amazing writers who build rich worlds, fully fleshed characters, and plotlines to rival any we see on the stage, screen, or page. Write on!

To the wonderful people at Split/Lip Press. Thank you for giving my words a home. You have been exceedingly kind and supportive on the path that helped put this book out into the world.

And a final thank you to anyone I may have unintentionally forgotten. I apologize and I love you.

About the Author

A native of Northeast Ohio, Athena Dixon is a poet, essayist, and editor. She is Founder of *Linden Avenue Literary Journal*. Athena's work has appeared in various publications including *GAY Magazine* and *Narratively*. She is a Pushcart Prize and Best of the Net nominee. A Callaloo fellow, a V.O.N.A. fellow, and a Tin House Workshop attendee, Athena is the author of *No God In This Room*, a poetry chapbook (Argus House Press). Her work also appears in *The BreakBeat Poets Vol. 2: Black Girl Magic* (Haymarket Books). Athena is the co-host of the New Books in Poetry Podcast via the New Books Network. She resides in Philadelphia. Learn more about the author at www.athenadixon.com.

Now Available From

Split/Lip Press

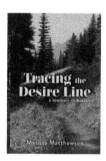

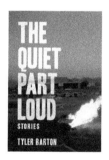

For more info about the press and our titles, visit

www.splitlippress.com

Follow us on Twitter and Instagram: @splitlippress

CPSIA information can be obtained
at www.ICGtesting.com
Printed in the USA
FSHW021949241120
76291FS